The Your Guardian Angel

PROTECTION

HEALING

ACCEPTANCE

TEACHING

SUPPORT

INSPIRATION

LOVE

REVEREND KIMBERLY MAROONEY

FAIR WINDS
PRESS

GLOUCESTER, MASSACHUSETTS

© 2003 by Fair Winds Press

First published in the U.S.A. by
Fair Winds Press
33 Commercial Street
Gloucester, Massachusetts 01930-5089

Library of Congress Cataloging-in-Publication Data available

ISBN 1-931412-39-1

10 9 8 7 6 5 4 3 2 1

Cover design by Laura Shaw Design
Design by Susan Raymond

Printed and bound in Canada

Dedication

To the Lord God Almighty for filling me
so full of His ways.

My eternal love and devotion to the
memory of Jim Marooney who taught me
how to give everything.

To Gordon and Ann for giving me
the courage to be personal.

To Paula, Edward, Lauren, Christa, Ilene, Charles,
and Iris from helping me to find the best in myself.

To Donna and Joe Robertson, my mom and dad,
for their loving support and Biblical scholarship.

To Dana Terrill. Thank you.

Contents

CHAPTER 1
Your Guardian Angel

*I believe we are free, within limits,
and yet there is an unseen hand,
a guiding angel, that somehow, like a submerged
propeller, drives us on.*

—Rabindranath Tagore, Nobel poet laureate

❧ Your Soul and Your Guardian Angel ❧

We are all cradled in the supportive and protective care of guardian angels. Our guardian angels are messengers from God, sent to guide us as we make our way through life. Each guardian angel has unique attributes. Your personal angel has the distinctive combination of qualities needed to help you lead a spiritually fulfilling life.

Think of your guardian angel as your loving companion who walks by your side, providing guidance and assistance. Simply believe that your angel is with you, as doubts will block your ability to receive the help being extended. Your guardian angel knows your needs so well that support is often presented before you even ask.

As your soul's best friend, your guardian angel may come to you as the nurturing presence of a mother to comfort you in times of need, bringing inspiration and beneficial influences. During crisis, your guardian angel may appear as a mighty catalyst, embodying the majesty and power of the Lord's love, prompting you to action. And in situations of physical or spiritual distress, your angel interacts with the strength and protectiveness of a father who pulls you swiftly from harm's way.

Most often, however, your guardian angel assists you in ways that are nearly invisible. With vigilance, you can begin to recognize the familiar, comforting feeling of your guardian angel's touch.

✦ Your Soul's Purpose ✦

Your guardian angel knows your soul's purpose. Your angel's primary concern is to strengthen your connection with your soul in order to bring your purpose into greater awareness. The soul contains the qualities you need to succeed in fulfilling your life's purpose. Qualities such as faith, courage, gratitude, determination, devotion, and love emerge to become dominant forces directing your life when you are connected with your soul.

Once you begin to actively seek your soul's purpose, your guardian angel becomes more involved in your life. The areas that do not support your soul's purpose are brought into awareness, and changes are initiated. During challenging moments, your angel offers revelations and incentives to encourage you to transform voluntarily. Perhaps new interests or inspiring friends help you to let go of conflicting ways of life without such a struggle.

As your life comes more into alignment with your soul's purpose your heart is filled with a love and a joy that has nothing to do with your circumstances. Relationships benefit from this love by becoming more intimate and satisfying. You feel as though you are in the right place at the right time. And when you celebrate life's victories, the radiant light shining on your success is none other than your guardian angel celebrating along with you.

❧ The Seven Gifts ❧

Guardian angels present many gifts to support the growing awareness of your soul's purpose and to develop the qualities needed to fulfill that purpose. This book introduces seven of these essential gifts in the chapters that follow.

The first gift is *protection*. Your guardian angel's top priority is to protect your soul's destiny, which is accomplishing God's will. You may feel overwhelmed and run in fear when you first become aware of God's will. Your guardian angel stays with you to provide everything needed to succeed at what God is asking of you. If you find yourself in physical danger and you still have work to do here on Earth, your guardian angel goes into action to keep you alive. You learn to trust God from such experiences, as you see your life from a new perspective.

The second gift your angel offers is *healing*. Your guardian angel helps you become receptive to the mighty healing power of the Lord through faith. As a divine comforter, your angel helps you to heal fear through love. During difficult times when you are beset with worry, your angel is there to help you gain control of your mind through prayer and endeavor. Your guardian angel also helps you learn to actively acknowledge the good in your life. Heartfelt gratitude is a form of devotion and a way to give back to your angel.

The angels play an important role in helping us find *acceptance*, which is their third gift to us. Your angel encourages you to face impossible situations realistically. When you are angry with God, your guardian angel helps you to transform the feeling into a passion for the truth. By discovering how your soul's purpose is involved, your angel can help you accept God's will. Then you can rise to the highest and best in yourself as you meet the situation with determination.

The fourth gift offered by your angel is *teaching*. Your angel is your teacher, instructing you about your soul's purpose, and helping you to recognize how you have been prepared for it. In addition, your guardian angel teaches you to recognize hints that are guiding you to the next step to take toward the fulfillment of your purpose. When you are off course, your angel guides you back to strength and happiness, not only helping you to renew your connection with God but also encouraging you to share this connection with others.

During dark nights of the soul, when you are in trouble and desperately need help, your angel is there with the fifth gift of *support*. At times like these, there is nowhere else to turn but to God. Your angel helps you to incorporate daily practices, such as prayer and meditation, which will keep you focused on the bigger picture so you can survive these precarious times. Your angel will also guide you to find the valuable association of people who understand what you are going through and can provide support. As human beings, we need human as well as angelic support.

The sixth gift from your guardian angel is *inspiration* to fulfill your soul's purpose. Through connecting with the truer parts of yourself, your angel helps you find your life's work. For some people, this feels like a specific calling to do God's work. For others, it is finding an attitude of love and devotion that can be applied to any task. Your guardian angel helps you to discern which desires are not in alignment with your soul's purpose. All of us are called to become God's partner in giving. Your guardian angel inspires you to answer the call.

The seventh and most important gift your angel brings is a more personal experience of God's *love*. And once you have been touched by His unconditional love, your angel helps you to find ways to share this love with others.

✧ A Closer Relationship with Your Guardian Angel and God ✧

How do you begin to receive the gifts of your angel? The desire to be touched by your angel's tender care and to know the personal love of God is the foundation for building this relationship. As you get to know your guardian angel, you are also getting to know God, and vice versa. As you learn about one, you learn about the other.

Your guardian angel is standing by, waiting for every opportunity to connect with you. You must be receptive to accept the love, direction, and comfort your angel wants to bestow. Exercises and tools offered in this book will help you become more open to your angel's gifts.

Journal writing is a powerful tool for self-awareness. Each chapter of this book suggests ways to reach out to your guardian angel in honest communication from your heart. In addition, you will be asked to contemplate questions that will help you find a depth of clarity and truth that will lead to greater understanding, acceptance, and love in your life. You will learn how to prepare this journal in chapter 2, "Angel Journals."

Prayer is the most powerful tool for communicating with your angel and with God. Your guardian angel will teach you to pray honestly and with the passion of your soul's desire. As you learn to pray, you become receptive to the many surprising ways in which God can answer your prayers.

You will also discover how to make prayer an active part of your daily life. Walking hand in hand with your best friend, your guardian angel, as you pray about questions, challenges, and desires gives your angel the opportunity to help you with all aspects of your life. Falling asleep at night in the embrace of your angel makes use of this precious time as your soul receives the comfort, guidance, and inspiration that will help you through the next day.

Meditation is another powerful tool through which you connect with your guardian angel and with God. During meditation, you have the opportunity to experience God's forgiveness, healing, and love. Meditation helps you get past superficial concerns to expose the depths of your soul. Love, trust, humility, devotion, surrender, courage, and inner strength are some of the qualities you'll find buried in those depths.

A benefit of finding greater openness and love during prayer and meditation is being able to share that love with the people in your life. Your relationships with family members and friends will become deeper, intimate, and more fulfilling as a result of what you learn from your guardian angel and from God during meditation and prayer.

Kindling the feeling of devotion as you create a shrine or altar for your guardian angel is another practice that will enhance this relationship. An altar can become a living part of your life when you intend it to become the meeting place with your angel. Take time each day to commune with your angel in prayer while you freshen flowers or plants, light a candle, and change the objects.

☙ The Connection Is Personal ❧

Because the connection with your angel and God is so personal, I am sharing some of my prayers and experiences to encourage you to become open to the intimacy of the relationship. Also included are a few powerful experiences and realizations people have shared with me through letters.

I developed a deep and direct relationship with the angels and God through my prayers. Many times, He answered my desire even as I was praying. Use my examples as inspiration to find honesty and passion in your personal communion through your own prayers.

My experiences were powerful teachers as I realized the gifts they offered. Each experience provided an opportunity to let go of counterproductive habits and uncover the truer part of myself, leaving me satiated by the personal love the angels and God have for me.

I encourage you to refer to my learnings as you grow from everyday experiences. Your feelings are the open door through which guardian angels can offer help. Say yes and take the loving assistance.

❦ Recognizing Interaction with Your Guardian Angel ❧

Personal experiences with guardian angels have one thing in common: You are changed. How have you been changed by the guiding influence of your guardian angel? Look back through your life, searching for the moments when your guardian angel succeeded in helping you to change. Forgetting these important occasions is one way of hiding from your destiny. Remembering these turning points with gratitude opens up possibilities to welcome more guiding light by building trust.

Change manifests itself in many ways. If you have been suffering through a difficult time, your attitude may shift as your guardian angel helps you to see the brighter side. You may bask in the comfort of realizing you are not alone.

Guardian angels love to introduce new influences by bringing you together synchronistically with others who have similar interests. An electric feeling of excitement and a sense of destiny often accompany these introductions.

Sometimes, you simply know something that you didn't know before. It comes as the answer to a question or the solution to a problem. This is a sure sign that your guardian angel is providing what you need to successfully fulfill your purpose.

The greatest benediction is to have your heart changed by divine love. God's love comes in an infinite variety of forms. It can be a tender, gentle caress to give comfort as you relax into the arms of the Mother holding you in love. Or, in times of profound life changes, the powerful love of the Father may pierce your heart with the courage and determination you need to keep going.

Trust the direction your angel is taking you, which is always deeper within yourself. Each situation will lead to a personal experience of God's love for you and your love for Him. The result of following this pull is always a feeling of more love, more freedom, and more peace.

∽ Exercise to Recognize Interaction with Your Guardian Angel ∾

Try to recall the many ways you have been changed as a result of receiving help from your guardian angel. Write about these instances in your angel journal. Read them for inspiration during challenging times. Use the following questions to help you remember.

❖ Was there an inner voice guiding you to the best choice in a difficult situation?

- ❖ Did a miraculous event save you from injury or death?

- ❖ Did an accidental injury turn into a Godsend as your life was changed for the better over time?

- ❖ Have you found greater faith as a result of severe challenges?

- ❖ Do you feel more love now after suffering a great loss?

- ❖ Have you received comfort in the darkest of times?

- ❖ Do you feel joy for no reason?

- ❖ Have things come together in a synchronistic way?

- ❖ Have you experienced a knowing that is beyond what you have learned?

- ❖ How are your prayers being answered?

- ❖ How is your guardian angel helping you?

Developing your relationship with your guardian angel will reveal the qualities of your soul. These qualities enhance life. They are already within you, waiting to be discovered. Your guardian angel is your mentor in this process of finding the truer parts of yourself so that you can fulfill your destiny.

Prayer to Dance in the Ecstasy of God's Love

My Lord, fill my heart that I may dance in the ecstasy of Your love.

Help me to go deeper and deeper into the power of Your presence

that it may carry me into the enthusiasm and opportunity of Your love.

I know that at times it will be difficult.

I know that it will stretch me beyond my comfort zone.

At times it will feel uncomfortable and intolerable.

I've watched others be stretched beyond what I thought was possible.

Each time they emerged in such unbelievable truth and beauty,

strength, love and compassion!

I pray that you do that with me today, Lord.
Stretch me beyond the limits of what I think is possible
that I may
dance in Your embrace of infinite variation and possibility;
of ever increasing, ever expanding love and ecstasy.
My lord, I pray, carry me away on the power of Your love
today
that I once and for all dwell in the wonder of the truth
with You.

CHAPTER 2
Angel Journals

"When we are mindful, touching deeply the present moment, we can see and listen deeply, and the fruits are always understanding, acceptance, love, and the desire to relieve suffering and bring joy."

—Thich Nhat Hanh, a Vietnamese mystic, scholar, and Buddhist monk

ᗧ Beauty and Devotion ᗡ

A journal is a place where you can reach out from your heart and soul in honest communication with your guardian angel. Its pages invite you to look at your outer and inner lives with a depth of clarity and truth that will help you to find greater understanding, acceptance, and love.

The journal itself is an important starting place. Find or make a journal that feels beautiful to you and inspires devotion. You may be able to find a blank journal with a cover that entices you to use it. If not, make this your first project of devotion, and create a book that is inspiring. Consider making a book cover to go over a blank journal. Another option is to use a three-ring binder with lined notebook paper.

Before you begin work on the cover, gather stickers, personal drawings, greeting cards, and magazines with pictures that interest you. Get a glue stick, scissors, and several pieces of paper to be the background.

Plan the cover size you need for your journal. If you are making a cover to wrap around a blank journal, think about how to make the cover fit well and stay on the book. If you are using a binder, get one with a clear cover that you can slip your design behind.

Once you have gathered the supplies you need and are ready to start, pray. Take at least 15 minutes to search for a feeling of your guardian angel. You may want to have a statue or picture of your guardian angel in front of you while you pray and work on your design. With devotion in your heart, ask your angel to help you feel the quality that will be the focus for your angel journal.

Be receptive to a response, then follow the direction you feel pulled in. Look through the collection of pictures or images. You will be attracted by certain feelings in the images. Cut out the pictures that draw your focus and begin to arrange them on the page.

The objective is to love the collage you are making and find pleasure from it each time you use your journal. There are no rules. Make it your personal statement of passion and devotion. It can include words, or not. Perhaps the cover will be just one image that you draw.

Keep your journal in a place that is convenient and private—perhaps near your bed in a dresser drawer or in your closet. You may want to keep it next to this book while you are working through the chapters.

❧ Write from Your Heart and Soul ❧

Journal writing is your personal way of looking within and communicating what is in your heart with your guardian angel. Your writing doesn't have to be a certain style. This is not a school essay, and you can't get it wrong. Spelling, punctuation, and sentence structure don't matter. What matters are the feelings and desires of your heart and soul.

This is your private space for working through feelings, issues, problems, and questions. It is also an invitation for you to explore your purpose in life and find ways to live it more fully. In this journal, you will look at your desires and decide which ones are important to focus on.

ᗱ What to Write About ᗰ

Here are some suggestions on what to write about: Write about how you feel daily. Write about what is wrong, what you are doing about it, and your realizations about what you are experiencing. What is going right? How are you fulfilling your purpose in life? Putting your thoughts and feelings into words by writing them down helps to empty them out of your mind and create space for the next topic.

Spend time each day recognizing the ways your guardian angel comes to you, provides you with information, guides and moves you. This is one way to cultivate your relationship. Pay attention. Write about how your questions are answered in life. How do you respond and take action when those answers come? Notice when you don't like how it feels. Write about those feelings, too. Find acceptance and move with it anyway.

When you are angry, vent your feelings. Just dump them out on the page uncensored. This is not the place to worry about the feelings of others. Write a letter to the person who is causing you pain, when you are suffering because of events in a relationship. Dump out your anger, hatred, hurt, unfulfilled desires, disappointments, betrayal, jealousy, sadness, and loneliness onto these pages. NEVER MAIL THESE LETTERS. They are only for you to release these feelings.

When you have finished venting, calm yourself. Then write about your contribution to the situation and actions you can take to let go of your anger and move toward reconciliation. What is the truth in the situation? What do you really need to tell the person involved? When you receive realizations, write them down. Then find more actions to take as a result of those realizations.

Another type of writing is to think through problems. Begin by stating the problem. Then ask questions and answer them. Let each question lead you closer to a solution. Look at the problem from many different angles. Don't just stop with your first thoughts. When you have something that feels like a solution, ask more questions about it. How would this solution impact your life? The lives of those you care about? How can you put it into action? Do you need to talk with someone about it?

Each chapter that follows guides you through how to write letters to your guardian angel and receive responses. In addition, you learn how to write prayers to your guardian angel and how to write about the responses you are receiving. You will also be guided toward how to write about realizations you receive and how to find actions to take.

❧ Contemplation ❧

Another form of writing is contemplation. Reader Bozena from Australia wrote to tell me a story from her life:

> "I remember as a tiny school girl being found by a nun in the church. I should have been outside playing sports. Fortunately, she was an exceptional woman and simply asked, 'What are you doing here?' I was terrified. It was against the rules and I'd been punished before.
>
> I remember my response clearly, 'I'm looking at God and God is looking at me.' My heart hammered; how would she react? To my immense relief and puzzlement she quietly said, 'That's contemplation, child,' and left. I remembered the word and years later looked up 'contemplation' and was satisfied. I've been a contemplative ever since and surely the angels were with me that day."

Contemplation is thinking deeply and thoroughly. In some spiritual practices, it is called mindfulness. Make it a practice to contemplate spiritual questions. Take time to look deeply within yourself for an experience of the truth.

Each of the "Gift" chapters that follow includes questions for contemplation. When you have a list like this, answer each question that pertains to you as completely and thoroughly as possible, then move on to the next question. Begin with these questions, then find your own. Keep a list of interesting questions for future contemplation.

Another way to practice contemplation is to devote 30 minutes to a single question. Think about it. Notice your feelings. Let your thoughts and feelings lead you to other questions. What can you find within yourself that is true? Are you open to receive an experience about it? What thoughts, feelings, and concepts are in the way of you finding more truth? What realizations are resulting from this contemplation? What actions can you take to use the realizations to change yourself?

Write notes from contemplations in your angel journal. Begin by writing the question, and then write what you are finding about it. Keep track of realizations and actions you will take to change.

When you do spiritual contemplation at bedtime, go to sleep with thoughts of God. Let the movement from your endeavor carry you all night. If you have time for spiritual contemplation in the morning, let the focus of your question be related to the upcoming events or issues of your day. Use the question to help you include God in your daily tasks.

༄ Important Discoveries ༈

You may want to keep a section in the back of your angel journal for important discoveries. When you have realizations that are important to remember, write them here so you can read them often and remember them.

As you work through this book, you will be writing powerful and personal prayers. Some, you will want to remember and use for a long time. Copy these prayers into a special section at the back of your angel journal so you can find them easily and read them often.

You will be guided to find action steps to take as you move through situations in your life. Some of these action plans will feel vital for your survival or fulfillment of your life's purpose. Keep these action plans in a place that is easy to find and where you have some room to write about realizations and successes that are the result of the steps you are taking.

When you have profound experiences in prayer, meditation, and life that are the result of your spiritual endeavors, write about them and mark the page so that you can easily refer to it for encouragement and inspiration.

This angel journal can become your most valuable friend. The more of yourself you put into it, the more treasure you will uncover within. Your guardian angel is your companion and guide every step of the way, so ask for help often. Over time, you will feel the touch of your angel on these pages.

Prayer for God's Love to Satisfy My Soul

My God!
Thank you, my Lord.
Help me to trust you and be open to receive Your love.
Love me, my Lord.
I am Yours to love.
My fear keeps pulling me away from Your love.
Your love is everything to me.
Your love fills my heart and satisfies my soul.
Your love tells me what to do.
Your love gives me clarity and direction.
Your love is Your will.
Your love helps me feel Your love for me
and my love for myself.
How You love us!
Your love teaches us how to love each other.
Love is all that matters.
Hold me in Your arms.
Cradle me in Your Love.
I am Yours.

CHAPTER 3

Gift #1—Protection

*For He shall give His angels charge of you to guard
you in all thy ways.*
—Psalm 91:11

✑ The Role of Guardian Angels as Protectors ✑

Guardian angels are best known for their role in protecting us from danger. As an example, a friend of mine named Ken was approaching an intersection while driving his car. The car suddenly drove itself into a gas station and stopped. A moment later, a semitruck with a trailer ran the red light and plowed through the intersection. The truck would have killed him if his car had not pulled over.

What are guardian angels protecting? For what purpose was Ken's life spared? Guardian angels are most interested in the destiny of your soul. Ken is convinced that his guardian angel turned the car into that gas station to give him a second chance to fulfill his destiny.

Most of the help we receive from our guardian angels is directing us toward the soul's purpose. What is the soul's purpose but God's will? For some people, God's will is a massive calling that consumes their entire lives. For most of us, our purpose is revealed one step at a time as we learn to become available to love each moment.

God provides everything we need to succeed in fulfilling our purpose and has appointed our guardian angels to be the project managers. When we are too afraid to seek God's will, our guardian angel patiently waits for opportunities to encourage us. If we endanger ourselves by running in fear, our guardian angels provide a rescue. And once we are ready to seek our purpose, our guardian angel protects us from our own negative thoughts and judgments as we learn to stay focused and trust God.

ᔕ Jonah and the Great Fish ᔕ

Jonah's experience is an extreme example of how we are protected as we struggle with choosing God's will over our fear. God told Jonah to go to Nineveh and tell the people that their city would be destroyed unless they repented. Jonah was Hebrew and the residents of this city, the Assyrians, were known and hated for their cruelty to Hebrews and other nationalities.

How would you react if God told you to go to a dangerous city and preach this kind of message? Jonah was quite disturbed and sailed on a ship headed in the opposite direction to get away from God and this madness.

ᔕ Running in Fear ᔕ

While at sea, a powerful storm came up that threatened to break the ship apart. The captain asked each man why he was there as they searched for the reason for this evil storm. When Jonah admitted he was fleeing the will of the Lord, the shipmates cast Jonah into the sea to appease the evil storm and save their own lives. It worked. The storm ceased, and the ship was able to sail on.

In the meantime, God prepared a great fish that swallowed up Jonah to save him from drowning. The waves washed over him. Weeds wrapped around his head. Can you even begin to image how the belly of a great fish would smell? The fish carried Jonah down to the bottom of the sea. The darkness of the deep closed in around

Jonah. For three days and three nights, Jonah lay in darkness and fear.

Eventually, even Jonah's soul fainted within him. At that point, he remembered the Lord and began a prayer of submission and gratitude. God was listening and directed the fish to vomit Jonah out onto dry land.

✎ Following God's Will ✎

This time when God told Jonah to go to Nineveh and preach the same message, Jonah went. As Jonah preached, people believed that he was speaking the word of God and listened!

When the king heard that his city would be destroyed if they didn't turn to God, he ordered a citywide decree that every man and beast should not taste anything, not eat or drink. During this fast, the residents of the city were to take off nice clothes and wear sackcloth and ashes while they turned from their evil ways and cried mightily unto God in humility and repentance.

What an amazing example of cooperation. Can you imagine the mayor of New York City ordering everyone to drop everything for a few days to carry out this extreme request—and then they do it? Millions of people fasting, wearing only burlap bags, sitting in a pile of ashes and wailing loudly for forgiveness? What a scene!

God was watching the sincere efforts of the Assyrians and spared their lives.

✄ Everything Needed for Success ✄

Many of the examples we have of God's will, such as Jonah's story, are fairly extreme. So, like Jonah, we run in fear when we hear God's will. Let's look more closely at God's will to work through the fears and find the truth.

What does God want for us? Does he want us to suffer and struggle? Is it God's will for us to be cruel to each other? No! God wants us to let go of our suffering and find love. He wants us to replace struggle with trust in His ways. God wants us to love each other in humility and devotion. God wants us to be His partners in caring for each other.

When God makes His will known, He provides everything needed to succeed. Jonah was a good example. God wanted Jonah to succeed at turning around the lives of the people of Nineveh. It would have been much simpler if Jonah had agreed when he received the first request.

Jonah's destiny was to go to Nineveh to deliver the message. When Jonah ran in fear, God stayed by his side and came up with some pretty interesting miracles to protect him, as well as provide what was needed at every moment to accomplish the task.

When Jonah was thrown into the ocean, this "prepared" fish was in position to swallow him, providing an environmental support system kind of like a minisub. While in the belly of this great fish, Jonah had to face immense fear of what God was asking, along with terror of the situation. Surely, Jonah's guardian angel was with him during this ordeal, providing comfort and guiding Jonah through the process of letting go of the way he wanted his life to be.

Jonah's prayer reached such a depth of surrender that he experienced being in the loving embrace of the Lord in the midst of such dismal circumstances. Overcome with gratitude, Jonah sacrificed his personal desires and vowed to follow the will of God.

God continued to provide everything needed for the success of this mission as Jonah walked into Nineveh. Perhaps the angels walked with Jonah, for as he spoke, not only did the people listen to someone they normally would have sneered at or even harmed, they believed Jonah and did exactly as he said.

How can this story apply to your life? Your destiny has to do with what God is asking of you. For some people, God is asking you to be a loving parent and partner. For others, it has to do with overcoming great adversity to build a life on gratitude and faith. And some may be asked to do outlandish things to create surprising changes for many people.

My friend Ken looked deeply at his life after the incident at the intersection. Eventually, he walked away from his wife and job to build a new life of devotion and service to the will of God. Now his trust in God's will is a great inspiration to many people.

✎ Exercise to Understand How Your Angel Has Protected You ✎

As a toddler, I fell into a swimming pool. My blanket that my little fingers were clinging to formed an air pocket around my face. When my mother saw the blanket in the pool and pulled me out, she was astonished. There was no water in my lungs. The blanket had acted like a life-support system, much like Jonah's "great fish."

It has been clear to my family and me since this incident that I have a destiny to fulfill. Like Jonah, I was fearful and ran from that destiny, making my guardian angel work diligently to keep me alive and pointed toward my purpose. But with each occurrence, I received more trust until I could finally join hands in partnership with God's will.

Have a conversation with your guardian angel about the nature of your soul's purpose and how you have been protected. Take at least 30 minutes for this exercise in awareness. Gather your angel journal, a pen, tissues, a pillow, and water. Make sure you can totally focus on this exercise and won't be disturbed. It may help to be in front of your angel altar. For more information see chapter 11, "Angel-Inspired Shrines and Altars."

Begin with a prayer asking your angel to be present with you and to help you find the information you need to know. During this prayer, move through doubts you may have that your angel is listening. You can do this through the sole quality of trust. Your soul already knows that your angel is with you.

Guardian angel,
Please be with me now.
Help me to recognize my soul's destiny.
I want to understand what you are protecting when
you care for me.
When I doubt that you are real, help me to find
trust in you.
When I try to run from my destiny in fear, help me
to find a courageous heart.
And when I have judgments about what God is
asking, help me to find the willingness to say yes.

Close your eyes and drop deep within. Keep going until you find an open heart and open mind. When you encounter fear or judgments, ask your angel to help you turn away from them to find a receptive mind and courageous heart. Search for the willingness to recognize the truth. You may want to refer to chapter 10, "Angel-Guided Prayer and Meditation."

Following is a list of questions to get you started in this conversation. Select the questions that apply to your situation. Remaining in a prayerful state, write a question in your angel journal and then answer it. Your soul knows the answers to these questions even if your mind does not.

Listen and trust the answers that come. Let the answers spark new questions that are unique to your situation, then answer those. Use the question-and-answer process to discover the information you need to know about your soul's destiny and how your angel is protecting you now.

- ❖ What is God asking of you?
- ❖ How is God asking you to have more love in your life?
- ❖ How is God teaching you to have more gratitude and appreciation?
- ❖ What should you be focused on?
- ❖ Do you have detrimental relationships or situations?
- ❖ Are you involved in a personal conflict that distracts you from what is most important?
- ❖ Are you involved in an abusive relationship?
- ❖ Do you cling to the wrong people because you are afraid to be alone?
- ❖ What is God asking you to change?
- ❖ How is this change protecting your destiny?
- ❖ How is your guardian angel protecting you now?
- ❖ How has your guardian angel protected you in the past?

❧ Letter Asking for Your Angel's Protection ❧

After you have finishing contemplating these questions, write a letter to your guardian angel. In this letter, tell your angel what you know of your soul's purpose. Then ask for help letting go of distractions so you can focus on your purpose. Ask your angel for help making the changes that are being asked of you. Thank your angel for the ways you have been protected in the past.

Write a personal prayer asking for your guardian angel's protection. Here is an example:

> *Guardian angel, protect me from inflicting*
> *judgments on others and myself.*
> *Protect me from my negative thoughts.*
> *Transform them into deeper love and care.*

Copy the prayer onto a beautiful piece of paper and place it on your angel altar. Each day, take the time to read your prayer and be receptive to a response from your angel. Write about any responses you receive in your angel journal.

⤳ Trust ⤳

It takes trust to accept the will of God. Guardian angels are our greatest example of trust because they live in a state of unconditional surrender and total trust in the will of God. In that state of union, they are open vessels for God's vast intelligence.

Through guardian angels, God is able to present a multitude of possibilities to us for each situation. Each possibility has the intention of helping us find more trust in His ways and more desire for His love. Every time you have that feeling of trust, you can be certain that you are receiving help from your guardian angel. Each time you have the courage to dive into the unknown, your guardian angel is standing by your side.

As you accept this type of assistance and begin to develop a personal relationship with your guardian angel, the feeling of trust emerges. Trust is a powerful magnetic force that attracts to you everything needed to bring your life into alignment with God's will. Trust is a natural quality of the soul because God's will is your true will.

God wants to shower you with the gifts of spirit: true love and care for yourself and others, higher intelligence to recognize truth and to make choices that will bring you more freedom in both the material and spiritual parts of your life, and gratitude and devotion to Him.

Trusting God opens the gate for you to step into the flow of His ways. Once in that flow, you are guided by His will. God uses guardian angels to introduce beneficial influences. You may have a profound experience or find a book that deeply touches your heart with truth. Perhaps you are guided to a group of people who affect you through powerful heart connections, increasing your desire for more intimate and satisfying relationships.

Through trust, you recognize that each experience in life has something to offer, especially the challenges. When the parts of your life are exposed that are in opposition to His ways, your guardian angel is protecting your soul's destiny. Relationships may break up, helping you to leave behind codependent and counterproductive ways of being. You may be laid off from work, giving you the opportunity to find a job that is more supportive of your emerging spiritual desires. Letting go of old ways opens space to attract people with similar spiritual desires and find new, productive, positive relationships. While the process of changing may be painful, a greater experience of love and freedom will result when you find trust and seek God's will.

Trust grows with experience. As an example, if you are in a relationship, each time the person delivers on what they said they would do, you have more trust in them. You learn whom you can trust with your tender feelings and most personal desires. With experience, you discover who has real care so you can trust that what they ask of you will be beneficial. Over time, you see who is telling you the truth. Trust is often a tangible feeling that is earned by delivering on promises.

You can build greater trust with your guardian angel and with God in this same way. Become vigilant at understanding how your guardian angel is delivering.

☙ Receiving Hints ❧

God is waiting to give us the information, direction, help, and love we need to fulfill our soul's destiny. God uses guardian angels to guide us through hints. Hints are subtle clues—like that little voice telling you things before you realize you need to know them.

Here is an example of a hint and how you can fully utilize what you have been given: Out of the blue, you think of a sentence in a book that could help your situation.

The moment you receive that hint, write it down so you don't forget. At the soonest possible moment, get the book and find the sentence. Copy the sentence onto an index card and begin to contemplate how its meaning can help you. Make a plan with actions you can apply to your situation from what you have learned from that sentence.

Find a feeling of gratitude and appreciation for what you have been given. Say a prayer of gratitude to your guardian angel. Gratitude and appreciation are simple ways to become more receptive to God's help. Gratitude is a magnetic force that attracts more of its kind. Gratitude is a quality of the soul.

Always be alert and vigilant for hints. Be prepared to receive them by having a notepad and pen with you so you can write them down. Don't assume you will remember. Be open to take action on them at the soonest possible moment.

For example, as you get in the car to go to work, you remember that you got a hint to find a specific sentence in a book while you were in the shower and you forgot to get the book. Get out of the car, go back in the house, and get the book. Find the sentence. Contemplate the message and use it to take action in your life that day. Give thanks.

Showing your guardian angel you mean business and are ready, willing, and able to act increases the flow. God wants to give us so much! He truly knows our needs before we do and tries to give us everything we need before we even know we need it.

Go to that place deep in your soul that has unshakable faith in God. Search for the openness to trust and receive before you understand. While our minds will never understand the mighty ways of the Lord, we can find the trust to say "yes."

❧ Exercise to Recognize Hints You Are Receiving ❧

What hints are you receiving? Set aside at least 30 minutes to contemplate the following questions. Write these questions and your answers in your angel journal:

❖ What hints have you recieved and taken action on? What was the result?

❖ What hints have you received that you didn't take action on and what will you do about that now?

❖ How can you be more prepared to receive hints from your guardian angel?

❖ How can you become more responsive to the hints you receive?

- ❖ How can you find more trust in where your guardian angel is leading you?
- ❖ Are you willing to act on God's will?
- ❖ How would your life change if you lived totally for God?
- ❖ What do you live for now?
- ❖ Can you trust God to provide what you really need?
- ❖ What would the Lord have you know?
- ❖ What changes do you need to make in your life?
- ❖ How can you become more receptive to your guardian angel's guidance through those changes?
- ❖ How would taking action on hints change your life?

After you have contemplated these questions, make an action plan. Find five steps you need to take based on what you found. For example:

1. Carry a notepad and pencil all the time so I can write down hints and take action.

2. Try an experiment: Do what the hints say and see what happens.

3. Schedule the time to make a list of the help I've received in the past to give me greater trust.

4. Every morning, sit for 15 minutes with my guardian angel and listen for guidance.

5. Take immediate action on that guidance.

Your guardian angel is dedicated to protecting your soul's destiny and providing you with everything needed to successfully accomplish what God is asking of you. That protection includes anything that distracts you from your purpose, from the smallest embarrassments to greater disturbances. When you are distracted, ask for the tender embrace of your angel to bring you back to focus. Look for the help. Seek it out. Take action on it. See how your life changes.

Prayer to Accept God's Help

My beloved angel,
please help me to stop resisting your help.
Help me to completely trust you.
What if I could let you move me without needing
to figure out why or where beforehand?
I am so stuck in wanting to know!
This is only because I am afraid.
What a relief it would be to not have to know everything!
Such freedom in not having to figure it out!
Help me to simply receive your hints with gratitude
and take action on them.

CHAPTER 4

Gift #2—Healing

"I have reached the point of not being
able to suffer any more,
because all suffering is sweet to me."

—Saint Therese of Lisieux,
a French Carmelite nun (1873–1897)

❧ The Role of Guardian Angels as Comforters ❧

Guardian angels are well known for their role in comforting us when we need healing from our afflictions. Whether those afflictions are physical illness or mental torment, turning to your guardian angel will help you find healing and greater love. Your guardian angel is a link with the mighty healing power of the Lord. There is an infinite variety to the form in which this healing power manifests. Love can be the antidote for fear, while prayer and endeavor may be needed to heal worry. And sometimes, the comforting embrace of the Mother cures our maladies.

As a child of nine years, Saint Therese of Lisieux became quite ill with a fever and was expected to die. Pauline, an older sister and nun with the Carmelite Order, came home to pray for Therese in her bedroom. Emulating her beloved sister, Therese also prayed to a statue of Mother Mary. Seeing Mary smile at her, Therese was healed. Therese went on to join the Carmelite Order at the young age of 15. Surely, her guardian angel guided Therese to the depth of her heart, where the healing love of the Mother was waiting.

Our guardian angels carry the loving comfort of the Mother and are standing by, waiting to embrace us. We are the ones who must become receptive. But how can we find receptivity? Faith is a powerful quality of the soul that can be the link through which our guardian angel guides us to the healing power of the Lord.

ৰ Become Receptive to Healing Through Faith ৰ

There are many stories in the Bible about the healing power that came through Jesus. In one story, a large crowd of people greeted Jesus. An important man in the town, Jairus, who was the ruler of a synagogue, fell down at Jesus' feet and begged Jesus to come home with him to heal his only daughter who was near death.

As Jesus tried to follow Jairus through the crowd of people, he stopped and asked, "Who touched me?" His disciples couldn't believe this preposterous question. How could they know who touched Jesus with this multitude of people pressing in? But Jesus persisted with the question because he could feel that something had happened.

As Jesus looked around, a woman stepped forward. Trembling, she bowed down before Jesus to declare that she had touched him. She went on to explain that she had been bleeding for 12 years. She had spent all her money on physicians with no success. When she touched the hem of Jesus' garment, the bleeding immediately stopped!

"And he said to her, Daughter, be of good comfort: your faith has made you whole; go in peace."

—Luke 8:48

As Jesus spoke with the woman, news came to Jairus that his daughter had died. When Jesus heard this, he instructed Jairus not to be afraid, rather to believe, and his daughter would be made whole. Arriving at the house, the family and friends who had gathered were crying and wailing the loss of the child. As he passed through the house, Jesus told the people not to cry. The child wasn't dead, only sleeping. The people laughed at Jesus in a scornful way, so Jesus sent everyone out except the parents and his own disciples.

Taking the child's hand, he told her to rise. Her spirit came back into her body and she sat up immediately. Jesus then instructed her parents to feed her some meat. Her parents were astonished!

In both of these situations, the people who were receptive through faith experienced healing. Had their guardian angels given them the courage to step out of the large crowd and come to Jesus? Probably. Our guardian angels are ever at our side, encouraging us to take actions that will result in deeper faith and healing.

After this episode took place, Jesus taught his disciples how to heal others with the power of the Lord and sent them out to the surrounding towns to offer this gift to the suffering people.

ᔅ Exercise to Ask Your Guardian Angel for Faith ᔥ

Faith is a powerful word that can help you to feel a deeper part in yourself. Have faith. Faith is beyond the scope of understanding. It is not connected with material life, but a presence that comes from spirit.

Can you feel a profound place within yourself when you say, "Have faith?" Close your eyes. Feel faith. It is a place within and a palpable energy. Faith is a key to the gateway into God's heart.

To recognize your faith, think about each of these questions and write about them in your angel journal:

❖ What experiences have you had that have given you faith in the Lord?

❖ How have you been healed through your faith?

❖ How have you benefited from the strength of your faith?

❖ Have you had experiences with your guardian angel that increased your faith?

❖ Have you had experiences when you felt something greater than yourself?

❖ Have you had moments of pure joy for no reason?

Write a prayer of gratitude to your guardian angel for these gifts and ask for experiences that will give you more faith. Copy the prayer onto a beautiful piece of paper and put it on your angel altar. Read it every day and watch for answers to your prayer in your life. Write about them in your angel journal.

৯৯ Healing Fear with the Power of Love ৵৵

At the age of 13, Saint Therese was an overly sensitive child who easily burst into tears. Even at this early age, she longed to enter the Carmelite Order for a life of devotion. Her prayers focused on how she could manage the strict lifestyle of the Carmelites when she was so prone to emotional outbursts. No answers came.

Then on Christmas Eve, only a few days before Saint Therese's 14th birthday, she underwent a profound experience of healing.

> On that blessed night the sweet infant Jesus, scarcely an hour old, filled the darkness of my soul with floods of light. By becoming weak and little, for love of me, He made me strong and brave: He put His own weapons into my hands so that I went on from strength to strength, beginning, if I may say so, "to run as a giant."
>
> —Saint Therese

During this experience, Saint Therese was healed of her fears and overly sensitive emotional reactions. After entering the Carmelite Order a little over a year later, she began to sign letters as "Therese of the Child Jesus."

I also received a powerful experience of having my fears healed through love. It happened as my husband, Jim battled with cancer before he died. He was overwhelmed with pain and unable to walk from the onset, requiring heroic care. The fact that he survived at all was a tribute to the grace of our guardian angels, giving us the time we needed to love each other deeply and say goodbye.

About two months into Jim's illness, I wanted to go away for a few days to a seminar. My request sparked a heated debate. Jim didn't want me to go and used examples from the past to point out how I tended to be selfish. That escalated to a temper tantrum where he broke down and cried! Jim never cried. He had always been calm and gentle with me.

I was beside myself. I went for a walk in prayer, begging my guardian angel and God to help me find the truth in this situation. Why was I so desperate to get away? By the time I circled around the block, I had received the answer to my prayer and was aware of my deeper feelings.

Jim was right. I was being selfish. I wanted to escape because I couldn't tolerate the pain of watching him die. My heart was being ripped to shreds and I was terrified of being left alone without him.

I went into the house and immediately confessed these feelings to Jim, with the prayer that we would find the truth together. He admitted that he needed to feel the strength of my love every minute that we had left. He was too vulnerable and afraid to be without me. He understood how I was feeling because he would escape too, if he could. My fear melted when he said that the only way he could tolerate the pain was with me by his side.

In that moment, I stopped wanting to run away. As we faced our fear together, it was replaced with a much deeper love and trust. With love in my heart, my fear transformed from the feeling of a concrete wall crushing down on me to one of a curtain of beads that I could pass through with very little effort by simply pushing the strands aside and walking through. That was a turning point where we found permission to voice all our feelings—no matter how ghastly they seemed—so we could work through them together.

Afterward, I had immense gratitude for this argument because our guardian angels had succeeded in helping us accept the horror of this situation by sharing our feelings. As a result, we were able to experience a love that was beyond anything we could have hoped for during the remainder of Jim's life. The satisfaction of that love was well worth facing the fear.

✧ Ask Your Guardian Angel for Healing and Comfort ✧

Most of Saint Therese's short life was filled with severe physical suffering from illness. Rather than focus on the suffering, she turned her mind and heart to prayer:

"I say very simply to God what I wish to say, without composing beautiful sentences, and He always understands me. For me, prayer is an aspiration of the heart, it is a simple glance directed to heaven, it is a cry of gratitude and love in the midst of the trial as well as joy; finally, it is something great, supernatural, which expands my soul and unites me to Jesus."

—Saint Therese, *Story of a Soul*

There are three main types of suffering: body pain, emotional pain, and mental torment. They go together so naturally that it is hard to tell them apart. Let's use a person who suffers from migraine headaches as an example. As the pain of the migraine become incapacitating, the person must stop all activities and retreat.

This opens up the door of mental torment, as the mind repeats phrases such as, "What if this is another five-day ordeal? I have to finish this project for the deadline! I've already missed so much work, what if I'm fired?" Angry feelings at being out of control of your body or life get mixed in. Memories of similar past experiences flood you, adding to the distress.

There is a simple way to gain control over this type of suffering. Briefly talk to yourself about the actual situation by asking the question, "What is true right now?" For example, "My head is in pain, my mind is spinning in negative thoughts, and I'm afraid. The only thing real is the pain in my head. The thoughts and feelings are imagined." Immediately let go of everything that isn't true.

When you drop out the mental and emotional elements, the physical pain may seem less severe.

The second question is, "What can I do about this right now?" Maybe stopping all activity to lie down with a pillow over your eyes will bring relief. Perhaps you can take a pain reliever. Take some kind of action to help yourself.

Once you have a grasp of the situation, turn to your guardian angel for help. Very simply, tell your angel what you have discovered. Ask to be held in the comfort and love of your angel's embrace. Then relax in trust and desire to feel a response. Each time you catch yourself worrying, return to your prayer.

You may feel the sweetest gentleness slip quietly over you, only to be snatched out by anxiety. Again, look for what is true and call to your angel to be held in love. In immediate response, a tender sensation washes through you, bringing relaxation.

You may go back and forth like this for a while before you can surrender to the comfort your guardian angel is offering. While your body may still be in pain, your soul can be embraced by the comfort of your guardian angel's loving presence.

◈ Gain Control over Worry ◈

Turning your focus to prayer is one way to step out of worry. You can also take action to gain control over your thoughts. Worry is persistent, negative thoughts that repeat themselves.

These thoughts fool you into believing that you are thinking because they are thoughts about problems. But each time you "think" about the problem, the same thoughts recur. These thoughts never solve the problem, nor do they advance your situation in any way. Worry follows a pattern:

❖ You repeat what you already know about the situation by describing what happened or defining the problem.

❖ You gather evidence to defend your feeling. You find other negative statements from experiences in your life to build a case to support the conclusion you have reached or the emotional position you have taken.

❖ You feel justified in having feelings such as blame or resentment because of the situation. This justified feeling can become righteous indignation. You are actually proud at being victimized by this situation and defend it.

❧ Exercise to Break through Worry ☙

Is worry capturing you with partial truths? Turn the tables. The first step is to listen to what your mind tells you. Carry a notepad and pencil and write it down. Ask your guardian angel to help you have the courage to see this part of yourself clearly:

*Dear Guardian angel, help me to become aware
of the negative thoughts controlling my mind.
Teach me to gain control of my thoughts and
stop worrying so I can find real solutions.*

The thoughts you write down may be something like this:

I'm always thinking, but my position never changes. My situation is impossible. Why do I make such bad choices? There must be something wrong with me. I am such a fool. Why do I listen to people who lie to me? I am dying of loneliness. Why am I so alone? I feel so lost. I hate my life. Everything is a struggle. Why does everything have to be so hard? I keep searching for answers that never come. I've made so many mistakes. I don't have anyone close to talk to. I feel hopeless.

There is hope. It takes determination and persistence to change negative thoughts. Worry is seductive because there is always some truth in it. The mind spins that tiny grain of truth into a whole scenario of failure. Look at the sentences you have captured like this:

❖ **Find the grain of truth.** "I'm always thinking, but my position never changes." Both parts of that are true.

❖ **What feelings does it trigger?** I feel stupid that I make bad decisions, I trust the wrong people. I don't have anyone in my life that could really help me. I feel hopeless, lost, and alone. I am frustrated that nothing changes. I am angry with God for not giving me what I want. I blame others for my bad situation. I feel angry that no one is rescuing me.

❖ **Do you generalize?** "I'm always thinking" is a general statement. Once you find the generalization, ask yourself questions like: Thinking about what? Am I thinking in a way that is productive or that can help? Am I asking questions about specific parts of my situation and then seeking answers? Am I trying to find people who are trustworthy and could help with my situation? Or am I repeating negative thoughts about past events and calling that thinking? "My position never changes." This is another generalization. Search for some truth: There must be some small change that happens. You should look to see specifically what has changed.

❖ **Think of five actions you can take to change.**
(1) My emotions are a powder keg. I could get on the exercise bike every morning for 15 minutes and blow those feelings out in the intensity of pedaling. Then I can start the day in an open and receptive state. (2) I could reach out to a friend who could support me in making positive change. (3) I could think about my situation and break it down into pieces. (4) Then I could focus on the most important piece first. (5) I could make that list of things that have changed in my life as inspiration and keep adding to it as new changes occur.

↤ Let Go and Move On ↦

After you have examined the content of what you are worrying about and found helpful actions, let it go. Decide to stop worrying. The letting go starts as a desire in your heart and becomes a shift in your attitude.

Close your eyes and imagine how different you would feel inside yourself if your heart were open and free to feel love. While you may not be able to change your circumstances for some time, how would your life change if you focused on positive, productive thoughts?

Focus on a bigger picture to find lasting change. What does God want for you? He wants you to turn to Him with your pain. God wants you to seek His love to fill your lonely, aching heart. He wants to comfort you and help you to find healing. He wants to guide you through difficult changes to find more truth and freedom. He wants you to seek His ways of love.

You don't have to heal everything to the point of being happy about it. For example, if you were in a painful relationship, you don't have to like the other person. Focus on letting go of your part and your intense emotions around the situation. The other person may not be very likeable.

Be serious and vigilant about this change. Each time you catch yourself worrying, remember the bigger picture of your desire for love and call to your guardian angel for help. Your endeavor is bringing change. Move forward and don't look back.

ᔍ Turning Persistent Thoughts to Prayer ᔥ

Turn persistent thoughts to prayer. If you keep asking yourself, "Why can't I let go of this?" catch yourself and pray, "Guardian angel, help me to let go of this."

From "I feel stupid and make bad decisions," pray, "Angel, help me to connect with divine intelligence so I can make accurate choices."

Instead of "I feel frustrated that nothing changes," pray, "Lord, give me the courage to make the changes you are showing me."

You may go through periods where a worried thought returns every five seconds. Negative thoughts will be the most intense right before a breakthrough. Each time you respond to a negative thought with a prayer, that is a success. If another negative thought follows your prayer, call on your guardian angel's assistance with more desire.

Don't be discouraged or give up. Your determination to succeed will eventually triumph, and worry will no longer be able to capture you.

ᔍ Exercise to Have Gratitude ᔥ

In the darkest moments, your angel is shining God's light on the suffering. To feel the love that your angel is holding you in, have gratitude. When you experience heartfelt gratitude, you are in the embrace of your soul.

No matter how challenging the situation, you can always

find at least one thing to be grateful for. Then find something else, and something else. Feeling gratitude opens you to be more receptive.

Change your focus during difficult times by writing in your angel journal about your gratitude. If you have a home to live in and food to eat, find gratitude that your basic needs are being met. Have gratitude for the people who care about you. Search for gratitude in the challenges you are facing, as gratitude will help you find the gifts being offered. And as a way of giving, have gratitude for your guardian angel's care.

To return your focus to gratitude frequently during a busy day, write the things you are grateful for on an index card in the morning and carry the card with you. Once every hour, take a minute to read the card and feel gratitude.

One of Saint Therese's biggest gifts to us is the gratitude and devotion she found in the little things of every day. Saint Therese's poor health left her able to perform only the simplest of tasks in Carmelite life. She turned each small task she did into a gift of loving devotion. "You know well enough that Our Lord does not look so much at the greatness of our actions, nor even at their difficulty, but at the love with which we do them," she said.

At the age of 23, Therese wrote her autobiography at the request of her prioress. Nestled among other stories rich with her mystical experiences, she tells how she learned to give to the fullest of her ability, while accepting her limitations.

Jesus set the book of nature before me and I saw that all flowers he has created are lovely. The splendor of the rose and the whiteness of the lily do not rob the little violet of its scent nor the daisy of its simple charm. I realized that if every tiny flower wanted to be a rose, spring would lose its loveliness and there would be no wildflowers to make the meadows gay.

It is just the same in the world of souls—which is the garden of Jesus. He has created the great saints who are like the lilies and the roses, but he has also created much lesser saints and they must be content to be the daisies or the violets which rejoice his eyes whenever he glances down. Perfection consists in doing his will, in being that which he wants us to be.

Jesus, help me to simplify my life by learning what you want me to be—and becoming that person.

—Saint Therese, *Story of a Soul*

This is how Saint Therese came to be called "The Little Flower." From early childhood, she had consciously aspired to become a saint, often assuring herself that God would not fill her with a desire that was unattainable. As Saint Therese suffered from tuberculosis and pulmonary hemorrhage near the end of her life at the tender age of 24, she found the inner strength to write many letters to family, friends, and other sisters of her order, as well as to continue work on her autobiography. Her little ways of giving to others transformed suffering into a state of loving communion.

∾ Rest in the Embrace of Your Guardian Angel ∾

Invite your angel to hold you in the healing presence of spirit when you are ill. Saint Therese showed us that, even during serious illness, it is possible to attend to the smallest details with loving devotion.

Resting peacefully helps to promote healing. What is disturbing you? Are you worried or anxious that you should be doing something else? Find a solution for the situation. This may be as simple as asking someone else to do that for you. Perhaps someone you work with can take over your projects. Or maybe your mother-in-law can care for your children.

If at all possible, make arrangements so you can rest without being expected to do anything else. It is easier to relax when the environment is clean, simple, and beautiful, with everything you need at your fingertips.

The biggest gift of illness is time for prayer and communion with your guardian angel. Let this communion be the natural expression of how you are feeling. Cry out your frustrations when you don't understand what is happening to your body. Talk through what needs to be done and ask for help. And rest in the comfort and peace of sweet love in your angel's embrace.

❧ Devotional Care ❧

Are you caring for someone who is ill? Find ways to care with loving devotion. Sick people often refuse help because they don't know what they need help with. They're sick and can't think clearly. You may be able to help anyway by suggesting specific things you can do.

Care for your loved ones as if they are precious children whom you have the pleasure and honor to care for. Don't expect acknowledgment or recognition. Let your giving alone be your joy.

Ask your friend's guardian angel to show you what needs to be done. Then look around and see what is most obvious. The angel will guide you. Perform each task as an act of loving devotion.

Begin with the area surrounding the bed and do some simple tidying up. Pick up used tissues on the floor and empty the trash. Is the tissue box empty and need replacing? What else needs to be replenished? Get fresh water in a clean glass. Straighten up the bed. Is the sick person hungry? Prepare something to eat. Freshen or throw away old flowers. Water plants. Feed the dog. Get the mail.

As an act of loving care, examine the items by the bed. What does your sick one need? Is something missing? How can these items be better organized so they can be easily reached? Clean the surface of the bedside table and remove anything extra. Arrange the needed articles so they are beautiful.

Evaluate the whole situation and think about how you can make your beloved one more comfortable. Perhaps there is a little dog that can't reach the bed and your loved one has to keep lifting the little pet up and down. Find a footstool or build a ramp with pillows so the pet can come and go without disturbing your beloved one.

As you spend time in the room, it will become obvious what needs to be done. Are there piles of things around the room such as laundry, bags of things, or stacks of mail? Wash dirty laundry. Fold and put away clean clothes. Sort through mail and move anything that doesn't need immediate attention to another room. Take stacks and bags of things away. When you look at something that needs to be done, you can't help but feel anxiety that you can't do it right now. Clear the room out as much as possible to create an open, welcome feeling of relaxation. Would your loved one enjoy hearing soothing music? If yes, how can you set that up?

As your loved one starts to feel better, change the sheets. What is the best way to help your friend freshen up? Simple things like brushing one's teeth make such a difference. Is your infirmed beloved weak and in need of help walking to the bathroom? Bring a warm washcloth for the face. Does the person need help taking a bath or shower? Wash and brush the person's hair. Help her change into clean pajamas. Remove old nail polish and clip or file nails. Tenderly massage lotion into dry skin. Give a foot rub. Help him shave.

Boredom can be a challenge during longer illnesses. Read a chapter in a book to your friend. Read get-well cards. Hold your friend. Watch a video together. Eat together. Help your dear one make a list of what needs to be done so the next visitor knows what to do.

Can you help with errands? Ask what videos to bring or return. Shop for groceries. Prepare several meals. Clean the kitchen or bathroom. Do laundry. Make a bank deposit. Pick up prescription medicine. Drive your friend to the doctor. Make phone calls. Look though mail for important items that may need attention. Help pay bills. Write thank-you notes to other caregivers or friends who have brought presents. Take the dog for a walk or to the groomer. Scan e-mails for items that need attention.

What thoughtful gift could you bring? Does your infirmed friend like flowers? Does she have a favorite ice cream or a particular kind of chocolate? Bring his favorite sandwich. Is there something you know would bring pleasure? Maybe a laughing Elmo stuffed critter. Could your friend use a small gift of money? Would a get-well card in the mail bring a smile?

As your friend recovers, help him or her get outside for a little sun when the weather is agreeable. Take a short walk together.

In all you do, have gratitude and care. Complete each task with a heart full of love and the joy of giving. This makes you a partner of guardian angels.

The Eternal Canticle

Exiled afar from heaven, I still, dear Lord, can sing,
I, Thy betrothed, can sing the eternal hymn of love;
For, spite of exile comes to me, on dove-like wing,
Thy Holy Spirit's fire of rapture from above.

Beauty supreme! My love Thou art;
Thyself Thou givest all to me.
Oh, take my heart, my yearning heart,
Make of my life one act of love to Thee!

Canst Thou my worthlessness efface?
In heart like mine canst make Thy home?
Yes, love wins love, O wondrous grace!
I love Thee, love Thee! Jesu, come I.
Love that enkindleth me,
Pierce and inflame me;
Come, for I cry to Thee!
Come and be mine!

Thy love it urgeth me;
Fain would I ever be
Sunken and lost in Thee,
Furnace divine!

All pain borne for Thee
Changes to joy for me,
When my love flies to Thee,
Winged like a dove.

Heavenly Completeness,
Infinite Sweetness,
My soul possesseth Thee
Here, as above.

Heavenly Completeness,
Infinite sweetness,
Naught else art Thou but Love!

—Saint Therese

CHAPTER 5

Gift #3—Acceptance

*"The ultimate measure of a man is not where he stands
in moments of comfort and convenience,
but where he stands at times of challenge and controversy."*
—Martin Luther King Jr., an American clergyman
and civil-rights leader who received the
Nobel peace prize in 1964. From *Strength to Love*

☙ The Role of Guardian Angels in Helping Us Find Acceptance ❧

Guardian angels have an important role to play in helping us find acceptance when we don't understand what is happening in our lives. Many experiences lack an element of fairness. It is natural to feel angry and abandoned during such times.

Your guardian angel can help you find patience to carry you through the ordeal. At some point, your guardian angel will help you to discover surprising gifts that are the result of those challenges.

Knowing that the situation is part of your soul's purpose helps with acceptance. Jesus was quite distressed over the coming events of torture and crucifixion that he faced. In the garden of Gethsemane, Jesus prayed with such anguish that "his sweat was like drops of blood falling to the ground" (Luke 22:44). He begged, "Father, if you are willing, take this cup from me; yet not my will but yours be done" (Luke 22:42).

As a result of his prayer, an angel appeared to strengthen him. When Jesus was satisfied that he must follow this destiny, he accepted.

In more recent times, Nelson Mandela spent 27 years as a political prisoner. When his mother died and he was not allowed to attend her funeral, Mandela turned inward to evaluate his own life. "Had I made the right choice in putting the people's welfare even before that of my own family?" he asked in *Long Walk to Freedom*.

He found strength from his answer, "In South Africa, it is hard for a man to ignore the needs of the people, even at the expense of his own family. I had made my choice, and in the end, she had supported it. But that did not lessen the sadness I felt at not being able to make her life more comfortable, or the pain of not being able to lay her to rest."

When Mandela was released, he was awarded the Nobel Peace Prize in 1993, then went on to be elected president in South Africa's first multiracial election in 1994. His destiny was clear and his guardian angel helped him find the courage he needed every step of the way.

As we find acceptance, our guardian angels help us to face impossible situations realistically. In this way, we can rise to the highest and best in ourselves as we meet the situation head on, saying yes to God's will and giving our whole self to the endeavor.

✦ The Trials of Job ✦

The story of Job helps to illustrate the trials we all endure. For most of us, Job's challenges help to put ours in perspective as being less extreme. The story begins on a day when the heavenly host of angels come to present themselves to the Lord. Satan was among them, so God asked him, "Where have you come from?" (Job 1:7).

Satan answered that he had been roaming the earth, and walking up and down in it.

God asked Satan if he observed His good servant Job, an honest and devout man. Satan observed that of course Job is honest and devout. God has protected him. Job became the wealthiest man in the East by pleasing God. He accumulated a huge estate of ten children, a large number of servants, and several massive herds of animals.

Satan suggested that Job served God only because he was profiting by doing so. What if Job were stripped of all his wealth? Would he still serve God, or turn away from Him?

God accepted the challenge, and Satan was allowed to inflict suffering on Job. If Job could endure the loss of his possessions and still serve the Lord, it would prove his integrity and vindicate the honor of God. Satan went to work.

∽ The Trial of Loss ∾

As we look in on Job, a messenger arrived with the news that the oxen were plowing while the donkeys fed beside them, when invaders murdered all the servants and stole the animals. He was the only survivor.

As this story was told, another servant came with word that "the fire of God fell from heaven," burning up 7,000 sheep and all the servants tending them. It seemed that lightning started a number of fires in the fields where the sheep grazed and it spread so quickly that none escaped—except this one messenger to bring the news.

While the tale of firestorms was being told, another servant arrived. Raiders in three bands ambushed the camel herders, killing them all and absconding with the camels. He was the only survivor.

Then a fourth servant interrupted with the most grievous news. All of Job's children were gathered at the house of the eldest son, eating and drinking wine together. A great wind came out of the wilderness and demolished the house. Everyone died.

At this, Job tore his clothes, shaved his head, and fell down upon the ground to worship, saying that he was born naked and when he dies, he will return to spirit naked. The Lord gives and the Lord takes it away. Blessed be the name of the Lord.

Have you ever felt like you were the pawn in a bet between God and Satan, as Job was? In the blink of an eye, all of Job's wealth was lost and his children were killed. Such devastation seems unimaginable and yet, it happens.

The families who were personally involved in the World Trade Center disaster must have felt just as devastated as Job. Not to mention the less newsworthy tragedy of families who are made homeless because of a lost job.

∽ The Trial of Sickness ∾

But wait, there's more. The next time the angels presented themselves before the Lord, Satan was again among them. God asked, "Where have you come from?"

Satan answered that he had been roaming the earth, and walking up and down in it.

God again asked, "What do you think of my servant Job? He still has integrity even though you made it look like I was out to destroy him without reason."

Rather than admit he was wrong, Satan taunted, "Yea, but any man will give up all that he has in exchange for his life. See what happens when Job is riddled with disease. Then he will turn against you."

God accepted the second challenge by saying, "Very well. Job is in your hands, just spare his life."

Satan left heaven and afflicted Job with painful sores from the soles of his feet to the top of his head. They itched so badly that Job scratched at them with a piece of broken pottery for some relief.

Job's wife tempted him to curse God so he could die and end his misery. Still Job refused by saying, "Shall we accept the good from God and not the bad?"

Job's sores were large pustules that disfigured him so badly that when his three friends came to visit and console him, they hardly recognized him. Even worse, worms and maggots were breeding in the sores, making Job reek with a nearly unbearable stench.

When the friends arrived, they sat down on the ground with Job. No one dared say a word for seven days and seven nights because they could see how great Job's suffering was.

Finally, Job could no longer endure the silence and the pain. In a passionate lament, he wished he had never been born; he asked the question, why does life continue when you are in such suffering? All of Job's fears manifested. He had no quiet or rest, just continuing torment. He couldn't even escape into sleep because of terrifying nightmares.

Eliphaz, one of Job's friends, attempted to comfort Job by suggesting that good people never die from suffering. This can't be accidental. Man is born into trouble, for that is his nature. All one can do is give everything to God. While God may inflict suffering, he also heals and eventually brings peace.

❧ The Trial of Anger ❧

Job was hurt that his friend didn't understand the situation. Bitterly, he complained to God about his suffering and asked to die. In this state, Job was struck by the immensity of this problem. Based on everything that happened to him, how could he continue to believe that God is just and wants the best for his children?

How could Job possibly defend his innocence against such a powerful opponent who was determined to prove his guilt? Job turned directly to God in a desperate attempt to understand God and why this was happening to him. That ended unsuccessfully in an even more despondent plea to die. Job was angry and hurt that God wasn't appearing as a witness to his innocence, vindicating him.

The three friends proceeded to gang up on Job with their belief that goodness is rewarded and that wrongdoing is punished. They bluntly accused him of some wrongdoing that he had not admitted and asserted that all of Job's suffering must be the result of this secret. They urged Job to confess it and all would be put right!

Job's claim of innocence endangered their simple beliefs. What if goodness isn't rewarded, but punished as is happening to Job? This was too disturbing, so the friends became angry with Job.

Anyone who has suffered through devastating health problems would love to be freed from such conditions by a simple confession. What if cancer could be cured by praying, "Lord, forgive me for cheating my business partner. I'll repay him and never do it again." Things are not so simple in our world. Neither were they for Job.

There are forces at work in our lives that we will never be able to understand. How can you ever understand why a passing car kills a beautiful four-year-old boy as he runs into the street after a ball?

∽ The Trial of Abandonment ∾

Isolated from God and his friends, Job pleaded for pity. At the depth of despair, something changed. Job had a leap of faith as he became certain that after his death, he would be able to stand before God to receive vindication. Job decided that his only hope was in seeking a response from God, even though God had been evasive and had appeared to be arbitrary in His actions.

Still, the Lord did not answer Job's appeals for intervention. The three friends intensified their attack on Job as they tried to coerce a confession from him. It became clear that they were unwilling to face the possibility that Job was innocent and his suffering was not the result of punishment for wrongdoing.

Job was shocked to realize how utterly isolated he was. His best friends became his enemies through their rigid beliefs. They could not comprehend Job's position, and they abandoned him. Even worse, the Lord deserted him and would not respond.

Turning to biting sarcasm, Job pointed out that the facts of life support the opposite position that the wicked are prosperous and peaceful while the innocent suffer. After burning out his rage on this tirade, Job lapsed into sadness as he mourned his former life of happiness and security and lamented his loss of respect and importance in the community.

☙ The Lord Appears ☙

Eventually, God replied directly to Job's repeated requests. When the Lord first appeared, Job felt he had the right to be angry with God for causing him to suffer without a reason; he wanted God to explain why this happened. At the same time, Job was deeply grateful because what he wanted more than anything was a personal experience of the Lord.

Rather than explain the situation, God lifted Job to a state of awe and reverence by showing him the wonders of divine creation in nature, changing Job's perspective to see as God sees. The majesty Job witnessed strengthened his faith.

Job's anger melted into humility as he admitted his ignorance and apologized. Faced with such glory and wonder, Job could no longer accuse God of being unfair and cruel based on his personal experience. Job accepted the fact that he could not understand God's actions, nor why the innocent are made to suffer. Job received deep comfort from his realization that God never abandoned him.

God then turned to Job's three friends to reprimand them for their behavior during this ordeal while commending Job for never faltering from his faith. God told the friends that if they would compensate Job with livestock and if Job would pray for his friends, God would not punish them.

After the exchange of prayers and livestock, Job was healed and the Lord made him twice as prosperous as before. All of Job's brothers and sisters and everyone who knew Job came to his house to console Job for the trouble the Lord had caused him. Each guest brought a gift of silver or gold. Job and his wife had ten more children and lived a very long life of prosperity and goodness.

∽ Finding Willing Determination ∾

So the story goes with Job, but it is seldom so clear-cut with us. How do we cope with uncertainty when everything we know is challenged? How do we discover the rewards of our endeavors when they aren't so obvious?

William James, the nineteenth-century American philosopher from Harvard, wrote "It is our attitude at the beginning of a difficult undertaking, which more than anything else, will determine the outcome."

Finding an attitude of willing determination in the midst of great challenge will help you stay focused on positive forward movement. When you don't understand what is happening to you, call upon your guardian angel to help you find acceptance. Your attitude about your situation can change even though you may need to be patient while the circumstances themselves run their course.

∽ Letter to Ask for Help Accepting Circumstances ∾

Write a letter to your guardian angel in your angel journal. Use this letter to vent your feelings of anger, resentment, victimization, bitterness, discouragement, and abandonment. Let the potency of these feelings drain out onto the page. Ask your angel to help you be expressive. Your guardian angel is by your side to help you dump out these harmful feelings so you can receive healing.

Next, write about your strengths. What qualities do you have that will help you with the situation? Willing determination can be one of those qualities. Write about your desire to let go of the feelings you spilled out in the first part of the letter. As you write, believe in your strengths. Willing determination can become your battle cry as you find a way to succeed when each new skirmish presents itself.

As an example, perhaps one of your strengths is a feeling of determination. You have no idea where it comes from; it just carries you through difficult challenges, no matter what. Or maybe you feel courage to keep going, even when you are afraid.

Tell your guardian angel how you will use your strengths the next time you are overwhelmed with the feelings you wrote about in the first part of the letter, like this: "The next time I am overwhelmed with anger, I will turn that feeling into determination to find a solution." Keep writing until you reach a position of strength.

Finally, write a prayer with that theme. Your prayer can be simple:

> *Dear guardian angel,*
> *The next time I am overwhelmed with anger,*
> *please remind me to let the anger become the*
> *determination to find a solution or acceptance for*
> *what I cannot change.*

When you have finished writing, sit quietly and listen for at least ten minutes. Listen for hints from your guardian angel. Be open to the presence of your angel. Over the next few days, listen for help and be alert for hints bringing what you need for your situation.

In your journal, write down the hints and inspiration you receive as well as the actions you take from them. Write about your realizations from these experiences.

✧ Defensive Strategies ✧

Let's look more closely at the dynamic of anger and victimization. When emotional pain is more than you are willing to feel, defensive strategies protect you from this pain. One strategy is to respond with anger or resentment and lash out at the other person. That can turn into an attitude of cynicism and bitterness. Another strategy is to withdraw and feel victimized. The feeling of wanting to die is not uncommon.

Let's use Job's experience as an example. When Job was severely challenged, his first defensive strategy was to feel victimized and to want to die. When he didn't die, Job's second defensive strategy kicked in as he became angry. His anger was a positive force that kept him alive. Job used his anger to speak up, essentially saying, "Look God, I'm a good man. You should stand by me."

The third defensive strategy was to become resentful and bitter when God didn't respond to Job's challenge. This was also beneficial because it opened Job's eyes to see a new level of reality in the world.

Unlike his friends who were still safe in their beliefs, Job was able to recognize that his belief system wasn't true. Good behavior is not always rewarded and bad behavior is not always punished. Job didn't have to look far to realize that bad people become wealthy while good people suffer for no reason.

Job's strength was his focus on the truth. His desire to discover the truth was the willing determination that pulled him through the ordeal by helping him to endure the suffering.

Job's guardian angel was there to transform his defensive strategies into greater awareness that kept him from giving up. And his angel pointed him toward God as he sought the truth.

ᔥ Exercise to Transform Challenges ᔥ

Each time you find yourself using a defensive strategy, your guardian angel is standing by to support you in finding greater awareness. What challenges are you facing in life?

Write about them in your angel journal. If your life is comfortable and peaceful right now and you don't have many challenges, great! Savor the experience and go on to the next chapter.

For the rest of us, begin by making a list. If you are dealing with big situations as Job was, your list may include things like a severe health crisis, a child who is struggling in school, a sudden change in your financial situation, or the pain of having a parent with Alzheimer's. Don't judge your list or compare it to anyone else's. This is a chance to be real with what you are facing.

Next, write a brief description of each challenge on your list. From those descriptions, select the challenge that you have the highest probability of effecting change. Write about this challenge in detail by selecting and answering the questions that fit your situation:

- ❖ What are your defensive strategies in this situation?
- ❖ Do you get angry?
- ❖ What are you angry about?
- ❖ How do you act out your anger?
- ❖ What do you say when you are angry?
- ❖ Whom does it affect the most?
- ❖ How do you feel about the impact your anger has on others?
- ❖ What do you resent?
- ❖ How does your resentment affect others?
- ❖ What do you say when you feel resentful?
- ❖ Whom does your resentment affect the most?
- ❖ How does your resentment affect others?

- ❖ How do you feel victimized?
- ❖ How do you behave when you feel victimized?
- ❖ What do you say to yourself about it?
- ❖ Do you feel abandoned or isolated?
- ❖ Whom do you feel abandoned by?
- ❖ What do you want them to do that they are not doing?
- ❖ What do you want from the situation?
- ❖ How is the situation stuck?
- ❖ What is your part in perpetuating the way the situation is stuck?
- ❖ Are you willing to let go of what you want so a solution can be reached?
- ❖ Describe the ways in which you are determined and willing to find solutions.
- ❖ Describe your strengths that will help you to keep going and not give up.

From what you have learned with these questions, write one clear sentence that describes your defensive strategy. As an example, "Rather than feeling angry and speaking up to find solutions, I feel victimized and resentful, dooming me to an isolated silence from the people I love."

Now it's time to call on your guardian angel for help. Write a prayer asking for change.

Guardian angel, please help me.
Teach me to speak up when I feel angry.
Help me to let the fire of my anger become a
passion for transformation.
I no longer want to hide feeling victimized
and resentful.
Give me the courage to tell the truth and find
solutions so I can have greater love with my family.

Write your prayer on an index card and carry it with you.
Read it every time you feel yourself go into this behavior.
Let your prayer and the care of your guardian angel guide
you to a deeper understanding of yourself.

❧ Exercise to Find Acceptance ❧

When you don't understand what is happening and the
circumstances are beyond your control, be patient. There
are some actions you can take to help yourself during
times like these.

Refer to your list of challenges in your angel journal. This
time, pick the one that seems the most impossible. Write
about your feelings and who is involved. Look at your
part in keeping this situation stuck. Are you hanging on
to the way you want it? Are you willing to find a different
solution?

Are you willing to have your perception of the situation changed, as Job's was when God appeared? Remember, God never answered Job's questions. God lifted Job into higher consciousness, changing his perception of the situation. In that moment, nothing was solved, but Job saw the problem differently.

It may be that way with you. If your mother has Alzheimer's, an improvement isn't likely. But you may find healing and greater love through prayer and acceptance.

Search for five actions you can take to change your perception of the situation and find greater acceptance. Using the mother with Alzheimer's as an example, perhaps she is living with you and you can't take adequate care of her. Your actions may focus on finding a small group home for people with Alzheimer's that offers compassionate care near your home so you can visit regularly. Or perhaps your actions are about letting go of your anger at the situation and the pain of not being recognized so you can find a new way to love her.

In each of these actions, seek the assistance of your guardian angel.

❦ Open to the Possibility of a Visit from God ❧

Guardian angels live for the moment when you feel a personal connection with God. That is their primary purpose. God does appear to ordinary people. Desire brings Him. Job's desire was strong enough to attract the personal presence of the Lord. You, also, can have a strong enough desire to attract a response from the Lord. God makes house calls.

God responds to persistent, heartfelt pleas. Job's situation was so dire that he was desperate. His prayers carried the depth of that desperation as a passionate desire for God to appear. Job was persistent enough that God finally answered.

Image a father who is working. As the father is seeing to the details of a very important business transaction, his little toddler is at his feet, pulling on his pants and jumping up and down with hands up saying, "Daddy, Daddy, Daddy, Daddy…" Eventually the father can't ignore the child another moment and lifts him up into an ecstatic embrace of love.

So it is with God. He is our Father and we are His children. He may ignore sporadic or halfhearted attempts to get His attention, but when we are persistent and determined, He must eventually pick us up into His embrace of loving ecstasy.

Pray with willing determination. Try different words and experiment with finding the deep feelings of your heart and soul. Your most powerful prayer may be simply, "Please!" Ask your guardian angel to show you how to pray so that God personally responds.

God seldom appears in a blaze of glory to reveal the answers to our questions. More often, He sends the Holy Spirit, which is His energy. You can feel it touch your heart. It flows like a river. Sometimes, it is tender like a gentle caress of your guardian angel. Other times it comes in a powerful blast as it washes away negativity. Allow the Lord to touch you personally in surprising ways.

Prayer for Illumination

Father, I am most afraid that You do not want me.
Yet You are desperately trying to show me the power
of Your love and the
strength of Your desire for me with experience
after experience.
More desperately still, I cling to my pitiful and
familiar ways of suffering,
letting the truth and joy of Your love and desire
be hidden by the darkness and lies of fear.
Enough!
The lies stop here and now!
My God, I beg You to illuminate my
consciousness with truth
until there are no dark places left for fear to hide.
Fill me with the power of Your presence, giving
me the awareness and fervent desire
to leave this prison of fear, never to return.
In You, I find everything my soul desires, my Lord.
I trust You completely.
Take me now.

CHAPTER 6

Gift #4—Teaching

"If I'm not (in a state of grace),
may God restore me to it,
and if I am, may He preserve me in it.
I would be sadder than anyone to know
I am not in God's grace!"

—Saint Joan of Arc, a French saint and
military leader, c. 1430

৶ The Role of Guardian Angels as Teachers ৯

Guardian angels play an important role in helping us to find our purpose. They do this by teaching us what we need to know to succeed in fulfilling our purpose. Each experience in life teaches us something important and our guardian angel is there, helping us to realize the lesson.

Your guardian angel sees a larger perspective that you do. Your angel knows your soul's purpose and is intimately familiar with your past and potential future. Using hints, your angel introduces influences intended to inspire you to make choices that will move you in the direction of your soul's purpose.

Even when aware of your purpose, it is easy to be distracted by the events of life. At such moments, your angel introduces bits of knowledge to help you see the distracting influences from a larger perspective. From this viewpoint, you are better able to concentrate on your soul's purpose.

Most important, your angel guides your return to strength and happiness when you are off course by helping you to renew your connection with God.

৶ Saint Joan of Arc ৯

Joan of Arc is an incredible example of receiving and following inner guidance. From being at her mother's feet during profound prayer as a young child, Joan learned to travel deep within. She was listening when her guidance came in the form of "voices." These voices taught Joan what she needed to know, consoled and encouraged her during difficult times, and guided every step of her short life.

The voices began when Joan was 13 years old. Walking from her house to the nearby fields, Joan passed the church when the noon Angelus bells rang. Joan devoutly recited the Angelus prayer in a state of sweet delight. Upon finishing the prayer, she heard a voice coming from the direction of the church, calling her name very distinctly.

Joan naturally turned toward the gentle and unusual voice. A great light enveloped her as she saw a majestic face surrounded by celestial beings. This first message began teaching Joan what she needed to know. The Voice said: "Be good and wise; love God very much. Go to church often!"

Joan was terrified by the voice and couldn't understand what was happening to her. Even so, a peaceful feeling filled her soul. Following this first experience, Joan decided to totally consecrate herself to God by taking a vow of perpetual virginity. She began to think of herself as Joan-the-Virgin.

∽ Joan's Preparation ∾

After several more experiences like this, Joan realized that the angel speaking to her was Archangel Michael. The voices came frequently over the next four years, preparing Joan for her purpose. During these conversations, Joan was carried into the presence of the angels and always came away with courage, confidence, and devotion. Joan never doubted that her voices were sent from God.

Great humility was a gift of this preparatory period. Joan never told anyone what was happening to her. She kept the secret and was never boastful or arrogant about being chosen for this special communication.

✌ Joan's Purpose ✌

At some point, the voices began to reveal Joan's mission. "It's you, daughter of God! ... It's you who will liberate France! ... Leave! Go to France! You must!" Joan was so overwhelmed and shaken by this impossible instruction that she replied in an anguished sob, "I am only a poor girl! I don't know how to ride a horse or to make war...."

Joan struggled with the pain of leaving her beloved family to carry out such an improbable task. Finally, the voices offered the encouragement needed to overcome Joan's fear with the words, "Daughter of God, go, go, go. I will be your helper. Go!" At the same time, a distant relative passed through town. Joan seized the opportunity and left with him.

Once out of her village, it took some time to win the support needed so Joan could proceed. Having been well prepared by her angelic council, she spoke the following words with such power and humility that she could no long be ignored and won that support.

> …Before mid-Lent I must be in the king's presence, even if I have to wear my legs down to the knees! Nobody in the world, neither kings, nor dukes, nor the daughter of the King of Scotland, nor anyone else can reconquer the kingdom of France. I'm the only one who can. I'd much rather stay with my poor mother, because this isn't my calling. But I have to go because my Lord wants me to.

Joan was provided with an escort and outfitted in soldier's armor for the trip to see the king. It took 11 grueling days on horseback, riding through dangerous country. As Joan overcame her own physical and mental challenges, she calmly assured the soldiers in her escort to not be afraid. It became undeniably clear that she was being sustained from a divine source.

Upon arriving at their destination, Joan and her escort were kept waiting for two and a half days while the king decided if her would see her. During that time, Joan prayed deeply and ceaselessly. When she was called into the king's court, she was taken into the royal reception hall, which was filled with lords and ladies and surrounded by 300 knights. Joan was fortified by the strength of her purpose as she overcame all obstacles of deceit, confusion, and distraction to convince Charles to put her to work.

✍ Fulfilling Her Purpose ✍

That was the beginning of her mission. Charles ordered a detailed investigation of Joan. The conclusion reached by the tribunal of theologians was favorable as Joan relentlessly answered their questions with precision and assurance: "I have been sent by the King of heaven, and I have voices and a council that tell me everything I must do."

By the end of this investigation, a long six weeks later, Charles was certain he could trust that with his soldiers, Joan would have the means to accomplish her mission. Joan was given the title of countess and provisioned with an entourage to guard, obey, and honor her. They would become her loyal and most faithful supporters until her capture.

Under Charles' order, Joan's little company was provisioned with equipment worthy of an envoy from heaven. Joan was outfitted in the finest armor and given a charger when it was discovered that she could ride well. Tall, strong, with thick black hair, she was a striking sight to behold in her shining armor and she inspired confidence in everyone.

When asked about a sword, Joan explained that God had provided one with five little crosses on it. It could be found abandoned near the altar in the chapel of Sainte-Catherine-de-Fierbois. Upon inquiry, the chaplains knew nothing about the sword. Nonetheless, a search was made and the sword was found just as Joan said, among other old and rusty swords and near the altar. After being carefully cleaned, the sword was sent to Joan.

A banner was made to fit a description given by Joan's voices. It would become an invincible rallying point of faith, love, and strength in the battles ahead. Joan later said, "I love it 40 times more than my sword!"

Once provisioned, the soldiers began to arrive at the staging area. Joan needed to win their allegiance and trust. The highest military commander gathered the troops and spoke in a thundering voice, swearing to follow Joan anywhere she lead. The soldiers were shocked to hear such a thing coming from their respected leader and took notice.

The foul language and rough attitudes of the men caused Joan great suffering. After speaking with the chaplain, Joan further declared that she wanted in her army only Christians who were at peace with God. As the soldiers listened to her, the result was astonishing. As they converted, it was as if they became as young as Joan was. Together, they were starting a new life.

Getting to this point was an inconceivable victory, yet the battle for Orleans lay ahead. Joan began by dictating a letter to the King of England, demanding the return of French land. When the English refused, Joan ordered her army to begin marching.

☙ The First Battles ☙

Approaching Orleans, Joan realized she was on the left bank of the river. Her voices had specified the right bank. "In the name of God," Joan said to the military leader who came to welcome her to the city, "the advice I receive from my Lord is wiser than yours. You thought you were deceiving me, and you deceived yourself. For I am bringing you the best help that has ever come to any city or general. It is the help of the King of heaven!"

The first battle for Orleans was won in a day, with a second victory following swiftly behind. Praying fervently in chapels whenever possible, Joan gave thanks for the victories and assistance.

The guidance that Joan received from her council was nothing short of miraculous. She was given intricate details about what would happen next and held firmly to the instructions given. Even when she was told she would be seriously wounded, she continued with courage and determination by telling her chaplain to stay by her side constantly the next day as she had much work to do.

The next morning, Joan got up very early. Following fervent prayer, she put on her armor and led the French to attack the fort of Les Tourelles. By midday, the French soldiers were exhausted. Joan seized a ladder and went into the battle at the walls of the fort. As she climbed the ladder, an arrow pierced her shoulder and she fell to the ground. Her soldiers quickly carried her to safety.

In great pain, Joan was afraid for the first time and cried. When a man offered to charm away her wound, Joan said angrily, "I would prefer to die than to commit a sin. The will of God be done! If anyone knows a remedy for my hurt, let him use it!"

As soon as she had spoken, Joan was touched by the presence of her voices and cried out, "I am greatly consoled!" She fiercely yanked the arrow out of her shoulder and allowed a compress to be applied as she tearfully confessed her sins.

The military leaders were gathered around Joan, assuming that the battle was lost. The order was given to sound the retreat. At this, Joan shouted, "In the name of God, I tell you, you will soon be entering Les Tourelles! When you see my banner floating in the direction of the fortress, take up your arms again. The day will be yours! Now, rest a little, drink and eat, get some of your strength back."

Never losing sight of her purpose, Joan remained focused on the situation and continued to care for others, even as she lay bleeding and in pain. While her commands were being carried out, Joan called for her horse and road out to the field with an open wound. She knelt in a short prayer that strengthened her. The knight who was holding her banner called to her with the news that the tip of the banner was toward the fort. Jumping on her horse and galloping into battle, Joan shouted, "Forward! Forward! Victory is yours!"

Carried by the miraculous force that surrounded Joan, the French soldiers rushed forward. The English, who had assumed Joan was dead, were shocked to see her and fled in panic. By nightfall, the fortress was taken. Church bells rang to celebrate the improbable victory as Joan road into the city. The next day, the English left and Orleans was liberated. This is how Joan came to be called the Maid of Orleans.

So it was that Joan was guided, protected, and comforted through all the challenges she faced both in battle and after her capture.

✧ Life Purpose ✧

A rare number of people have huge destinies that are made known very early in life, like Joan's. For most people, the purpose for life is more gentle and simple. It is centered on learning to be compassionate, courageous, truthful, forgiving, generous, caring, loving, focused, and determined. And, within those qualities, to be open to receive the loving direction of your guardian angel, guiding you into God's will.

Joan's words clearly express the nature of this relationship. The voices of the council that she heard and the visions she saw were from saints and angels who were directing her to follow God's will. Joan never lost sight of the fact that God sent the help. She was deeply grateful to the saints and angels who supported her, and to God, from whom the help originated.

During the preparatory period, Joan's guardian angel instilled such a passionate and vital faith in Joan that it sustained her through the darkest times and her execution. Her faith never wavered.

You can think of your purpose as the recurring theme in your life. It is your central desire. It may have variations, but it remains basically the same. For example, my life purpose is to find complete union with God and to serve His will by helping others to have personal experiences of His love. That is the central recurring theme in my life.

Each time I make a choice, I ask: Will this bring me closer to God? Or take me further away from Him? Is this God's will? I experience my purpose as a driving force within me that never lets me forget. It is a relentless feeling and a desire.

My purpose has unfolded step-by-step. Each step is the next thing that is in front of me. Often, these things seem to have little to do with my life purpose. But when I relent and face them, the realizations I receive as a result are surprising. And when I make choices that end up taking me away from God, I turn my direction back toward His love.

❦ Exercise: How Has Your Angel Prepared You? ❧

Joan began her mission as a simple peasant child who couldn't even ride a horse. Her voices taught her and provided everything needed for her mission. No doubt Joan's guardian angel was quietly working behind the scenes to coordinate the assistance of Saint Catherine, Saint Margaret, and Archangel Michael.

Like Joan, you have been taught and guided through your life toward your purpose. Write about these questions in your angel journal:

❖ What skills have you learned?

❖ What experiences have guided you to greater meaning in life?

❖ What personal experiences have you had with God and with angels that revealed your purpose?

❖ How are your skills and experiences coming together?

❖ What qualities, such as courage, fortitude, faith, determination, and compassion, have you received that sustain you through difficult challenges?

❖ What hints have you received about your mission?

❖ What do you know about your purpose?

✦ Letter to Ask Your Angel about Your Purpose ✦

Once you have gathered what you know of your purpose, ask your guardian angel to reveal more. Ask your angel questions based on what you discovered about your purpose. Write the questions above in your angel journal, then sit quietly and listen for an answer.

Write down feelings and thoughts you have. It may seem as if you are just talking to yourself. Notice everything you are receiving without judgment. Let yourself be open and receptive. Think about what you received. What did it tell you?

When you find a particularly powerful and potent question, write it on an index card and carry it with you. Give yourself a few weeks to explore various answers to this question. Be open to receiving many different perspectives on this question.

Watch for hints in your life that relate to the questions you asked. Your guardian angel loves to introduce new influences through friends, strangers, your own thoughts and feelings, and dreams, as well as by guiding you to information in books. Perhaps you hear a song that deeply moves you in a direction of wanting something. That is a hint. What do you want? How does that relate to your purpose?

You may want to keep all your questions, notes, and insights on your purpose together to help you see how your skills and experiences are synchronizing to fulfill your purpose.

∽ Exercise to Find Your Next Step ∾

Your guardian angel uses simple parts of life most effectively to guide you in your purpose. What are you facing? What do you need to focus on next? The next step is the thing that is right in front of you. It could be a great challenge or a persistent nuisance.

Take the time to tend to it as if it has some pertinence to your purpose. What is it telling you? As you focus on this next step, ask your guardian angel to help you discover what God wants. When you are in the flow of God's will, miraculous things can happen.

As an example, perhaps your financial situation is a bit messy because your expenses are greater than your income. You haven't known what to do about it, so you haven't done anything. Over time, it has gotten worse.

What if your purpose had something to do with your financial situation? In researching other employment options, you could discover a job that becomes your purpose in life bringing you great fulfillment and also solving your cash flow dilemma.

In your angel journal, write about the following questions:

- ❖ What is your next step?
- ❖ How has your guardian angel prepared you for this next step?
- ❖ What options do you have?
- ❖ How will each option bring you closer to your purpose?
- ❖ What do you need to learn more about?
- ❖ Do you need help? If so, who could help you?
- ❖ What actions can you take?

Write a prayer asking your angel for help to discern God's will in this next step. Copy that prayer onto a beautiful piece of paper and place it on your altar. Each day that you are focused on it, sit before your altar and pray, talking to your angel. Listen for how your guardian angel talks to you. It may not be through hearing voices as Joan did, but your angel's method of communication will become apparent if you persist. Write down insights you receive.

Watch for hints in your daily life that relate to your prayer. Write these hints in your journal to keep track of them. Find ways to take action on them and write about the results of those actions. Write about what you are learning about your purpose.

Describe the relationship that is building with your guardian angel in your journal. Show gratitude by giving thanks to your angel for the help you are receiving. Perhaps put fresh flowers on your altar. Taking action on the hints you receive is the best appreciation you can show your angel.

✧ Receiving Hints through Dreams ✧

Dreams can be a tremendous source of inspiration and information. Occasionally, dreams are literal. I had a dream that a friend looked me deeply in the eyes and said, "I am so lonely!" It was a profound dream. When I woke up, I was disturbed about it, so I called the friend and scheduled a lunch date.

We hadn't talked for a while so we began by chatting about life. Then I told him about the dream. He confessed it was true. He was feeling a very heavy loneliness. Our friendship provided some comfort.

Our guardian angels had gone to work to bring my friend the support he needed. My angel reached me with the hint to contact him through a very specific and real dream.

Other dreams are more symbolic. There is a story in the bible about Joseph and his coat of many colors. Joseph's brothers were jealous of him and sold him into slavery.

The Pharaoh of Egypt, where Joseph was imprisoned had two troubling dreams. After failing to find an interpretation of these dreams, the Pharaoh learned that Joseph had such a gift and sent for him.

Joseph attributed his insights to God and took no personal credit for them as he explained that through these two dreams, God was warning Pharaoh about what was to come. There would be seven years of abundance followed by seven years of famine.

After this interpretation, Joseph suggested that the pharaoh appoint a discerning and wise man to collect one-fifth of each harvest over the next seven years to store up so that they would have enough food to survive the famine. This plan was so brilliant that the pharaoh put Joseph in charge, by restoring him to wealth and giving him a wife—setting him up for this new life of power and importance.

Joseph's prediction came to pass. There were seven years of abundant harvests, and then the famine began. Joseph opened the storehouses as planned and sold the stock-piled grain to the Egyptians.

The famine was widespread, and all the countries around Egypt were devastated. As news of the grain spread to these starving people, they came from other countries to the storehouses. Joseph's brothers, who had sold him into slavery, came for grain as well. The family was reunited. Joseph revealed that coming to Egypt had been God's purpose so that he could save many lives.

Joseph's guardian angel knew the purpose of his life. Joseph had unknowingly been prepared for this purpose from childhood by learning the skills he would later need. It may have appeared that Joseph's life was off course when his brothers sold him into slavery, but Joseph's guardian angel was with him all along, protecting him through the experience of imprisonment and continuing to teach Joseph what he would need to know. Then at the appointed time, the angel provided the needed insight so that many people could survive the famine. Joseph was returned to strength through his connection with God. The result was the happiness of being reunited with his family.

✧ What Do Your Dreams Tell You? ✧

When you fall asleep at night, think about the questions you are exploring about your life purpose. Ask your guardian angel to provide insight and encouragement through your dreams.

In the morning before you get up, remember your dreams. When they contain information or hints about the questions you ask and your requests in prayer, write about what you are receiving in your angel journal.

Based on what you are learning, find actions that will move you closer to your purpose. Have gratitude to your guardian angel.

✍ When You Are Off Course ✍

It is easy to get off course from your purpose. As soon as you realize this has happened, pray about it. The fastest way to rediscover your purpose is to renew your connection with God.

Ask your guardian angel to help you find the way back on course by helping you to feel God's love. This can happen instantaneously, or it could take determined effort. There are so many things you can do to attract a direct experience of God's love and His will for you!

Talk to your angel by writing in your angel journal. Ask specific questions that will help you work through your current situation as you turn toward your purpose. You can take walks with your angel and talk about the situation. Go to sleep in prayer begging for help. In the morning, sit up in bed and take the time to recognize the help you received during the night.

Listen for answers and watch for hints in your life. Pay attention to hints you are receiving through your dreams. Take action on the help you receive with gratitude. Search within yourself for faith that you are being guided. For encouragement, look through your journal and find evidence of the help you are receiving.

Draw on your strength to help you find the truth in your situation. Use your next steps to steer toward your purpose. As Joan of Arc said, "Help yourself and God will help you."

Your guardian angel is by your side, helping you to experience God's personal love for you and your purpose. You will succeed in returning to strength and happiness as you align your life with your purpose.

I've Been to the Mountain

Like anybody, I would like to live a long life—
longevity has its place.
But I'm not concerned about that now.
I just want to do God's will.
And He's allowed me to go up to the mountain.
And I've looked over and I've seen the Promised Land.
I may not get there with you.
But I want you to know tonight, that we as a people,
will get to the Promised Land.
And so I'm happy tonight;
I'm not worried about anything;
I'm not fearing any man.
Mine eyes have seen the glory of the
coming of the Lord.

—**Martin Luther King Jr., American clergyman and**
civil rights leader, April 3, 1968. The next day, he was
assassinated. From *A Call to Conscience: The Landmark*
Speeches of Dr. Martin Luther King Jr.

CHAPTER 7

Gift #5—Support

"When we are flat on our backs there is no way to look but up."

—Roger W. Babson, businessman and statistician (1875–1967)

✺ The Role of Guardian Angels in Providing Support ✺

Guardian angels have an important role to play in supporting us through dark nights of the soul. During times that seem beyond endurance, your guardian angel tenderly holds you in an embrace of compassion. Your angel's main focus is to provide you with the support needed to help you endure unconscionable experiences as you question everything you know and lose faith.

Your angel provides influences that will support you in making positive choices each step of the way through this time of uncertainty. Influences may come in the form of a caring friend who sits with you through an impossibly painful night. Or a single word may pop into your mind that gives you the faith needed to take the next tiny step.

Regardless of the way these influences arrive, you can be assured that your guardian angel is doing everything possible to support you through the rough patches in our lives. The goal is to survive and grow from the experience. Along the way, you gain a strength of maturity that is forged in the fires of God's love. Your tears temper the steel that becomes your courage, determination, humility, trust, and ability to take action.

✺ Surviving Despair ✺

I managed to survive a lengthy dark night of the soul with the support of my guardian angel. The day my husband, Jim was diagnosed with cancer, my life changed radically.

My dark night began after he died and lasted nearly two years.

During Jim's illness, the house was full of people. His brother Mike moved in with us, and his parents arrived early every morning and stayed until late at night to be with Jim and to help with his care. The friends who loved Jim streamed through the house all day, checking in on him, coming to be with him, bringing love and little gifts of things they knew he liked.

After Jim died, Mike moved out, leaving me suddenly and utterly alone. No daily visits from family, no stream of friends, just me. The house that had been so full of love and life was shockingly desolate and dead.

A depth of despair and pain gripped me that I had no idea was even possible. It seemed I would die if I felt that pain. My life seemed devoid of everything but suffering as the love I had known with Jim drained out of me. In this state of despair, the ample supply of morphine left over from Jim's treatment came to mind. I began to think how easy it would be to take enough morphine to never wake up again.

✧ Finding Desire ✧

My desire for the eternal love of God kept me alive during this period of suicidal despair. That desire told me what to do each step of the way through my recovery from the grief of losing Jim. My guardian angel helped me to take those steps.

The night that I wanted to die, I knew I needed help immediately. When my best friend, Michelle, popped into my mind, I called her and said, "You have to come and get me right now!" It was about 10:00 at night and she lived 45 minutes away. We made a plan for how I could survive those 45 minutes until her arrival. I took only a toothbrush and pajamas to her house that night. My guardian angel was on the job, introducing the thoughts and influences needed to keep me alive.

By the next morning, it was clear that I should not go home and be alone. I needed to be with loving and supportive friends. Michelle brought me home to get my car and a small suitcase of clothing. Several days later, I returned home for a large suitcase of personal things and never again slept in that house.

My desire to find the eternal love of God guided me. I knew I had to quickly let go of the life I had shared with Jim. I put the house up for sale and took only what I needed. My mom sold everything else in a garage sale while I cried in the bedroom. Working overtime, my guardian angel attracted a buyer for my house and belongings in a very short time, so that I was able to move on and begin to build a new life.

Through my church, I was given the volunteer job of caring for one of our ministers by cleaning his home and shopping for groceries. This simple task of giving took me out of myself and provided spiritual support. Periodically, the minister would ask how I was and answer questions with helpful advice.

The next time I wanted to die rather than feel this pain of separation, I called on my guardian angel:

Please help me to find the courage to keep going.
I am willing to face anything to feel God's
eternal love.
Show me the way.

⤜ Receiving Help ⤝

Deeply disturbed one day, I took a long bath to think about why I was so unhappy. Rather than relaxing me, the feelings intensified. I cried to my guardian angel, desperately begging for a breakthrough.

Please, help me to see into the core of my
unhappiness and give me the courage to
move through it.
Show me how to be free of the suffering I am in.

As I prayed with intense desire for a response, the thought popped into my head to do something that was diametrically opposed to the feelings that overwhelmed me! I splashed cold water on my face and went shopping for some sexy clothes. The mood was lifted! This was a much greater breakthrough than I could have hoped for.

A plan of action emerged. I made three signs. The first sign said, "Give yourself what you need." This experience showed me that when I took the time to satisfy my needs, I was rewarded with feelings of joy. My heart lightened up and life was tolerable.

The second sign was, "Reveal the truth." I discovered that when I was willing to feel my emotions, they could change quickly. In this way, my guardian angel was touching me with the grace of God.

The third sign said, "Completion." I had been continually overwhelmed by all the tasks that needed to be done. My emotions were so raw that it was impossible for me to think clearly. I didn't seem to be making progress on anything.

As part of the plan of action, I got some big art paper and made a chart listing each task with boxes for the progression of steps that went with each. From that master chart, I could see what was most urgent to do next.

Then I made a list of what I completed each day so I could see that I was making progress. Each time I checked off an item, I felt just as elated as when the teacher put a star on my paper as a little child. I can still envision the silver stars she used. With everything so clearly and simply displayed, the feeling of being overwhelmed lifted. I thanked my guardian angel for providing such powerful assistance.

✄ Facing Pain in the Arms of Your Guardian Angel ✃

Several weeks later, I had a profound realization. I could allow my guardian angel and God help me in a much more personal way than I had ever thought possible. The feeling of not wanting to live had been terrifying to me. I had been trying to avoid it any way possible.

Now I realized that I could go into that despair with my guardian angel holding me! I could ask for help completing the tasks of material life. I had been shutting out my angel and trying to do it myself. That was why it had been so difficult and burdensome. That realization brought a surge of joy and gratitude. It was also a powerful turning point that led to more realizations for dealing with despair:

❖ Don't confuse things you have to do with letting go inside. You don't have to conquer the material world to fall into God's arms of love.

❖ Give yourself time to heal. There is a natural unwinding process. Give yourself the space to be.

❖ Don't be in such a hurry to rush through grief. Be willing to hang out in the uncomfortable feelings.

ꙮ Letter to Ask Your Angel for Help with Despair ꙮ

Write a letter to your guardian angel in your angel journal. Tell your angel about your feelings of despair. Use despair as a diagnostic tool, exposing what needs to change in your life. The first step in helping yourself is to determine the cause of your despair.

Write about these questions in your letter:

❖ What is wrong?

- ❖ How does this relate to your deepest desire?
- ❖ What is missing in your life?
- ❖ What have you been praying for?
- ❖ Could these feelings be how God is answering your prayers?
- ❖ What are these feelings telling you?
- ❖ Are you feeling overwhelmed and, if so, what is causing this feeling?
- ❖ What do you know needs to change?
- ❖ How can you begin to make that change?

After you have looked at the problem, think about your strengths. What quality do you have that keeps you going? Ask your angel to help you find this quality within yourself.

My quality is willingness. I can always find the willingness to keep moving toward God. God has been so responsive to my prayers that I can find the willingness to trust Him, no matter what I am going through.

Look deep within yourself to find your quality that will always pull you though difficult moments. Everyone has one quality they can turn to. If it does not immediately pop into your mind, ask your guardian angel to give you a hint so you can find this quality. Write about it in your angel journal. Describe how this quality has helped you in other situations. Explain how it is helping you now.

Next, identify your desire. What are you passionate enough about that it will keep you alive in the darkest moments? For me, that passionate desire is finding the eternal love of God. What is it for you? Are you passionate about your tiny child and will do anything to keep going for that child? Perhaps your love for your mate is incentive. Maybe your work pulls you through because of the satisfaction you receive.

Write a prayer of gratitude for these gifts of passionate desire and the quality of strength you have found. In the prayer, ask your angel to help you be more aware of your desire and this quality so you can receive greater benefit from them.

With a feeling of appreciation and devotion, copy the prayer onto a beautiful piece of paper. You may want to decorate it in some way. Place the prayer on your altar and read it every day during this difficult time. Be watchful for responses to your prayer in the form of hints, dreams, realizations, experiences, and inner knowledge.

☙ Seek the Grace of God ❧

Even in the darkest of times, there is a place within you that is serene. Do what you must to find this feeling of forbearance. It may be very tiny and remote at first. Focus on it and let it expand. It is the grace of God and is a benediction of your soul.

Ask your angel to help you obtain this grace. Standing in line at the store, turn inward so grace can trickle through you like a silver stream of sunshine. Driving in your car, put on music that inspires the flow of a stream of grace to wash away your weariness and distress. At home, set aside 15 to 30 minutes for meditation. Play music that pulls you into a profound connection of grace with your guardian angel and be renewed.

Grace may feel calm and clear. Or like a soldier, coura-geous and poised for battle. Let its qualities fill you and carry you through the pain. From this place you can turn the corner into joy.

Seek out this place often. You may only be able to feel it for a moment at first. Be patient and search again. With persistent practice, it will become easier to find and keep this feeling of grace.

ᔆ Get the Help You Need ᔓ

Despair can be dangerous to your physical, emotional and mental well-being. Take it seriously and get the help you need to work through it. Assemble a team of people to support you. Talk with family members and friends who can help you move in positive directions. Choose the ones who can encourage you to find the questions and actions you need to solve your problems. Don't turn to those who are negative and will pull you down ever further.

Your physical condition may require medical help. If you are in despair longer than three weeks, see your doctor to investigate physical causes. You may need psychological counseling for a period of time. Get the care you need.

☙ Exercise to Make an Action Plan ❧

Make an action plan to counter your challenges. An action plan is an organizational system to help you stay focused on what you need to do. Not being focused leaves you vulnerable to the influences of fear, confusion, and being overwhelmed. A survival plan like this needs to be balanced, including items from all areas of your life.

During dark nights of the soul, focus on the next thing that must be done. Make your life as simple as possible by thinking about what is essential. What responsibilities and tasks are not essential and can be eliminated? How can you organize the essential tasks for success?

☙ Personal Care ❧

Begin by thinking about what you need for your basic personal care. When you neglect yourself, then hate your reflection in the mirror, you will feel even worse. In your angel journal, write about these questions to discover what you are neglecting:

❖ Are you getting enough sleep? If not, why not? Think of actions you can take to improve the quality of sleep so you are more rested. Go to bed earlier if you have been staying up very late. Stop drinking beverages with caffeine and alcohol. Wind down before bed by writing about your feelings in your angel journal. Pray as you are falling asleep and ask your guardian angel for help. If this is a serious problem, get medical support.

❖ Every day, take a shower and dress so your strengths show through. It is quite temping to stay in "comfortable" clothes when you are at home all day. Resist the temptation and make the effort to look good for yourself. Do it as an act of devotion to yourself. On challenging days, talk to your guardian angel every step of the way, searching for your qualities of strength and desire to carry you through. If you are very ill, at least wash your face, brush your teeth, and comb your hair.

❖ Do you brush your teeth every day? Do you need dental care?

❖ Are you exercising? Exercise can help break through despair. Use intense cardiovascular workouts to burn up emotions by having the intent to let go and move on. Exercise can be anything that works in your situation. You may need to be creative to find the type of exercise, the time, and the resources needed. Ask your guardian angel to guide you.

❖ Is your diet supporting your body's needs? Does the food you eat make you stronger? Or do you get sleepy and feel worse after eating? Do you skip eating or overindulge? How can you set up an eating plan to support a healthy body and mind? Plan grocery-shopping trips. Make a list of simple foods that make you feel alive and buy only what is on the list. Plan cooking times into your schedule. If you tend to go for fast food, pack a lunch and take care of yourself. Ask your guardian angel to help you find simple and effective ways to eat well.

❖ Do you need a haircut? It is common to neglect your appearance during bouts of despair. Get a haircut.

❖ How do you feel about your appearance? Do you feel old and depressed when you look in the mirror? Get a makeover. Update your hairstyle and color. Go to a department store where an expert can suggest different makeup options.

❖ Are your clothes frumpy and depressing? Be creative in finding ways to dress beautifully, even if that means you have only two good outfits. Wear one while you wash the other.

After you have explored these areas and identified your weak spots, begin your action plan by finding ways to attend to your basic personal care as a tool against despair. Do you need a daily chart to tape on your bedroom door that has the tasks you forget to do—like brush teeth, comb hair, shower, dress well, exercise, eat—and then has boxes for you to check off each day? Get stickers so you can reward yourself each time you complete a task.

Consider a second chart with the one-time items such as getting a haircut, going through your clothes, and making appointments with a dentist, nutritional consultant, makeup expert, and personal trainer. As silly as it may seem, simple tools like a chart with appealing stickers can be the little sparks of motivation that make the difference.

⤎ Areas of Responsibility ⤏

The next area to think about is your commitments. Are you overwhelmed by tasks that need to be done? How can you stay focused on the most important things? Just as you did with personal care, go through your areas of responsibility and make a list of what needs to be done.

Which areas are you neglecting the most? Perhaps you haven't balanced your checking account and checks are being returned. Is there a mountain of laundry in your closet and you have nothing clean to wear? Maybe your car is out of gas, filthy, and embarrassing to drive.

Once again, charts may be helpful to keep you focused. Consider organizing the list of responsibilities into projects, weekly tasks, and monthly tasks. On a monthly calendar, schedule the best times to complete these tasks. Check them off for some satisfaction after you have completed them.

Your list may be long and feel overwhelming. Prioritize the tasks by when they need to be completed. Which tasks are not essential and can be eliminated? Can you delegate anything? Once you have a general plan for completion on a monthly calendar, think about what needs to be done today.

ᗌ Spiritual Practices ᗌ

What spiritual practices will help you to focus on the bigger picture? Ask your guardian angel to help you choose the practices that will be most beneficial. Consider including daily prayers, meditation, writing in your journal, and reading books in your daily activities. You can also take daily walks with your angel. See chapter 12, "A Walk with Your Angel."

Giving to others can transfer your attention away from your suffering. When consumed by despair, it is natural to become self-absorbed and lose your perspective. Giving from your heart can help pull you through into an experience of love. This breaks open the despair—at least temporarily—so you can feel some joy. Treasure those moments as the grace of God fills you. Plan ways to give to others.

ᗌ Make Signs ᗌ

During acute distress and despair, you forget everything you know and cannot help yourself. Despair often goes in cycles with several weeks in darkness, followed by some relief with lighter feelings. The despair returns when you least expect it, catching you off guard and leaving you utterly devastated and unable to remember what you have learned.

As you have realizations and moments of clarity, you will know how to help yourself. Make signs from the information you receive that can be your lifeline during moments of devastation. Here are some examples that have helped me.

When I am devastated by despair, I am completely overwhelmed by feelings of confusion. My mind generalizes by lumping many different things together into unmanageable and impossible pictures. I cannot see the truth in each unique situation. As an example, "I lost all my savings." In truth, I lost part of my savings, but not all. While feeling victimized, I couldn't think clearly enough to salvage what was left and make better choices. This sign helped me through this feeling:

> It is not true that everything is unworkable, unmanageable, and confused. Focus on the truth.

Another trick my mind plays when I am lost in despair is to repeat stories of my past experiences over and over. In that way, I apply past pain to current situations and don't really notice what is happening now.

> How are my past experiences and stories blocking my awareness of the truth now?

ᔆ Exercise to Make Signs ᔕ

The signs can be realizations, quotes that are deeply meaningful to you, or instructions to yourself of what to do when you forget. Anything from a sticky note to an 11″ x 14″ piece of paper with colored pens will work.

Identify the most difficult places in your home, then take action to help yourself in those areas.

Looking in the mirror can be torturous when you see your suffering reflected back at you. Write notes on your bathroom mirror with makeup pencils. Choose words that bring comfort and help you to feel loved. I was traveling alone in Central America during the September 11th terrorist attacks. All international flights were canceled indefinitely. Not knowing when I could return home was a very traumatic feeling. In my hotel room, I wrote expressions of love in large letters on the mirrors. With mirrors all around the room, it made a substantial difference to feel surrounded by love.

Going to bed alone at the end of a relationship can bring up brutal feelings. Put a sign of comfort and encouragement on the floor by your bed, telling you what you need to remember as you go to sleep. Getting up in the morning may also be a difficult time. Put a sign on the floor to remind you what to do first thing in the morning to begin the day.

Put sticky notes in your daily planner and on the dashboard of your car. Write inspirational quotes on index cards and carry them with you. Make a sign for your kitchen table to address the pain of suddenly eating alone. Read your signs often, especially during the darkest times.

ᔕ Turn to God ᔐ

Despair is a necessary part of the spiritual path. When despair is accompanied by the realization that nothing in your life truly satisfies, a greater longing opens up within. This longing is God's hand reaching out to pull you home. God's eternal love lies on the other side of the despair. All you have to do is turn the corner to come into the love. Your guardian angel can make it can happen in an instant when your longing is focused and intense.

Don't force anything. Let your guardian angel guide you through thoughts, feelings, and events. Opportunities will present themselves so you can rearrange your life to be more aligned with your true desires. Take action on the hints you receive from your guardian angel.

When you break through these darkest of times, you come into brilliant light and union with your angel and God.

ᔕ Association ᔐ

It is tempting to cut yourself off from others and retreat into seclusion when you are in despair. Instead, find others who have similar interests and want mutual support. If you don't belong to a church or spiritual group, create your own group. Search for several others who have similar spiritual desires and meet regularly in your homes.

This type of association is vital to create an environment of safety so that you can find more deeply loving relationships with each other. Take the time to develop trust so that you can share deeply personal feelings and let your heart open in vulnerability. Coming together with others in serious devotional desire encourages the qualities of the soul to emerge.

As a group, contemplate spiritual questions. Meditate or pray together. Read books and discuss what you are learning. Support each other in making life changes. Share realizations. Bring in guests or speakers to present new information. Search for experiences of truth and love.

In addition to group association, find a spiritual buddy for additional personal support. A good buddy listens without judgment and does not confuse the ugly, dark feelings you share with who you are. The buddy encourages change and can give positive feedback and encouragement, rather than reinforcing old ways of suffering.

What kind of buddy are you? How can you change to be stronger and more supportive to someone else? How can you go deeper within yourself to find the truth your buddy needs to hear? Do you have the courage and the strength to stop your buddy from gossiping or complaining?

❧ Confidentiality ❧

With both spiritual groups and buddies, have respect for each other. Keep everything that is spoken in confidentiality so that it is safe to expose your deepest feelings and be vulnerable without the worry that what you said may be used against you in the future.

Don't gossip about what you heard. Once you leave a group session, don't bring up what was said behind someone's back. At times, gossip disguises itself as discussing a situation to help the person. Don't be fooled. Talk directly with the person involved and no one else. Be mindful of your responsibility to uphold the safety of the relationships.

Refrain from making comments outside the group to someone about what they did or said during a group. If help was requested, offer your help in a way that is clear, straightforward, and mindful of the person's feelings.

∽ Exercise to Find Association ∾

How do you find people with similar interests if you don't currently have association? Approach your desire as if you were searching for a new job. Pray about it. Ask your guardian angel to help you.

Make an action plan to keep your attention on the endeavor. Your desire is the magnetic force that will attract you to others with similar spiritual desires. Remember to be open to receive hints so your guardian angel can guide you to the people you seek.

In your angel journal, write about questions like these to help you discover what you want:

- ❖ What are my spiritual desires?
- ❖ How can I find others with similar desires?
- ❖ What kind of spiritual support do I want?
- ❖ What kind of friendships and relationships do I want?
- ❖ How can I have deeper conversations with the people I know about spiritual desire?
- ❖ How can I find the trust to be more vulnerable and talk about my spiritual desires with the people I know?
- ❖ Where can I look for spiritual support?
- ❖ Who do I know that I could speak to?

It could be as simple as asking your friends if they pray or meditate. When they say yes, ask what they do for spiritual support. Do they belong to a group?

If your friends aren't helpful, look in a local newspaper for listings of spiritual groups. Try out a number of different types of events. Look at flyers and brochures in the places you go, like bookstores and health food stores.

Don't give up if your search isn't immediately successful. Find greater desire. Ask your angel to help you be more specific about what you want to find with others. Be more specific in your prayers. Are you listening for hints? Are you taking action on the hints you receive? Are you making judgments that you can't do that? Are you thinking it will never work? Are you afraid?

When doubt or fears come up, you are in association with your guardian angel. Your angel is acting as your spiritual buddy to reveal the areas that need your attention. Do your part to work your way through what you are being shown.

You may have received a hint to ask someone at work if they meditate, but you were too afraid to ask. Your fear stopped you. You could make a list of what you fear: rejection, termination, or humiliation. Then pray for courage and ask.

With the caring support of family, friends, professionals, spiritual buddies, and your guardian angel, you will survive your dark nights. Once you emerge, you'll find new strengths and qualities that resulted from being forged in the fires of love and tempered with rivers of tears. Ask your guardian angel to help you discover these strengths and qualities.

Francine wrote to me that, "I'm in some trying times right now, but I have had to search for answers because of them. And gratefully, I am finally dealing with many issues that will make my future much more joyful."

Prayer of a Lost Fool

Hold me, Lord.
This fool is lost again.
Hold me in Your arms of love that I may
find the courage to
plunge deeply into the pain within my broken heart.
It is the pain of separation from You.
It is the greatest of all pain and the most precious.
This pain draws me ever closer to You.
When I relent and feel this pain, it is such a relief!
It takes tremendous effort to keep it away,
yet feeling it is what I want the most!
It is my doorway to You!
How blessed I am to know this pain so well.
What a fool I am to fear it and avoid it.
I am Your fool, my Lord.
In Your mercy, have no mercy on me and
do what you must
so I can submit to the pain and ride it home to
Your tender embrace!

CHAPTER 8

Gift #6—Inspiration

"There is always the danger that we may just do the work for the sake of the work. This is where the respect and the love and the devotion come in—that we do it to God, to Jesus, and that's why we try to do it as beautifully as possible."

—Mother Teresa, a missionary in India and Nobel Peace Prize laureate, in *A Gift for God*

❧ The Role of Guardian Angels in Fulfilling our Purpose ❧

Your guardian angel plays an important role in helping you fulfill your purpose through your life's work. One way the angels do this is by helping you to discover the truer part of yourself.

The soul's desires are a link to the truer part of yourself. These desires are the magnetic force that attracts what you need to fulfill your purpose. And when you are distracted, your guardian angel helps you sort through your desires so you can focus on the ones that lead toward your purpose.

Another way your guardian angel helps you to fulfill your calling is by teaching you to give wholeheartedly and with joy. In this way, any job can become your life's work—even cleaning bathrooms, when you do it as an act of loving devotion.

❧ Mother Teresa of Calcutta ❧

A moment of clarity struck 17-year-old Agnes Bojaxhiu as she received her first calling, realizing that the purpose of her life was to teach and work with the poor in India. Agnes's mother was shocked by this announcement and disappeared into her room until the next day. By the time she emerged, she had accepted her daughter's decision and gave her full support. Investigating the options available for Agnes to pursue this endeavor, they came across the Sisters of Loreto in Ireland, who trained nuns to teach in India.

The training in Ireland was a mere two months of basic nursing and English, and then Agnes was off to Calcutta. She took her vows as Sister Teresa, named after and inspired by the "little ways" of Saint Therese of Lisieux.

World War II broke out, and along with it came the Great Famine of 1942 where two million people died. Mother Teresa managed to continue her work in the convent, centering her days on teaching and prayer during these cataclysmic times. Father Celeste van Exem entered Mother Teresa's life during this time, becoming her spirtual advisor.

Two years later, Mother Teresa was preparing herself for retreat as she rode the train to Darjeeling. The poverty she had seen as she lived sheltered in the convent, the hungry children, and the people living and dying on the street had made a powerful impression.

Clearly, as if someone were speaking directly to her, Mother Teresa heard the order that she was to leave the convent to live and work among the poor.

"God wanted me to be poor and to love Him in the distressing disguise of the poorest of the poor," she said, according to *Mother Teresa: A Pictorial Biography*, by Joanna Hurley.

Leaving the safety and support of her convent was the most difficult part of Mother Teresa's path. However, the call was so strong and clear that she did not hesitate, even though it was unheard of for a nun to live and work outside a convent and the association of an order.

Father van Exem believed her vision came directly from God and supported the proposal, beginning the process of receiving permissions. It took two long years, and the approval of the pope, for Mother Teresa to become the first nun in 300 years to receive such permission. During the process, Mother Teresa remained confident that God would put her where He wanted her to be, and tell her what to do once she got there.

∽ Faith That the Answers Will Come ∾

Mother Teresa did not know how or where to begin. She had only the faith that answers would come. She began by planning one step at a time, an approach that would last her entire life.

It was clear that to work among the poor, Mother Teresa would need some basic nursing skills and that she should dress as the Indian women did. This decision was the first step. The pace of life in the convent had been slow. Now, however, events happened with lightning-fast rapidity.

Dressed in her new habit, a white sari trimmed in blue, she left for Patna to study nursing at a missionary hospital. After only four months of training, it was decided that she should go to work immediately and the help that was needed would come to her.

A small allowance was provided from the Sisters of Loreto when Mother Teresa returned to Calcutta. Living in the Saint Joseph's Home for the Poor, Mother Teresa went into the worst slums of Calcutta and gathered together a few desperately poor children. Sitting under a tree, amid streams of raw sewage, she began to teach them rudimentary reading, writing, and hygiene.

✺ God's Work ✺

Mother Teresa's empire emerged from this simple beginning. Later, when interviewed for *Time* magazine, Edward Desmond asked, "Humble as you are, it must be an extraordinary thing to be a vehicle of God's grace in the world." She replied, "But it is His work. I think God wants to show His greatness by using nothingness."

When asked if she had any special qualities, Mother Teresa answered, "I don't think so. I don't claim anything of the work. It is His work. I am like a little pencil in His hand. He does the thinking. He does the writing. The pencil has nothing to do with it. The pencil has only to be allowed to be used."

Mother Teresa always assumed she could do what was being asked of her. She never let anything stop her, often begging on the street for what was needed next. Over her long life of service, she would become a symbol of selfless giving and a living saint. The Missionaries of Charity, which she founded, has more than 445 houses in the poorest areas of the world, with over 3,000 nuns to provide shelter for the homeless, food for the starving, medicine for the sick, and comfort for the dying.

These words from Mother Teresa express how her mission has grown:

> When once a chairman of a multinational company came to see me, to offer me a property in Bombay, he first asked: "Mother, how do you manage your budget?" I asked him who had sent him here. He replied: "I felt an urge inside me." I said: Other people like you come to see me and say the same. It was clear God sent you, Mr. A, as He sends Mr. X, Mrs. Y, Miss Z, and they provide the material means we need for our work. The grace of God is what moved you. You are my budget. God sees to our needs, as Jesus promised. I accepted the property he gave and named it Asha Dan (Gift of Hope).
>
> —Jaya Chaliha and Edward Le Jolym, *A Guide to Daily Living with Mother Teresa: The Joy of Loving*

↶ Letter to Ask Your Angel to Help You Find the Truer Part of Yourself ↷

Your purpose is a link to your soul. Each time you tap into your purpose, you are feeling the truer part of yourself that emanates from your soul.

By focusing more of your thoughts and energy on your purpose, you are inviting your soul to be more present in our daily life. The benefits of this involvement include having direct experiences of the many qualities of the soul such as faith, determination, courage, and love.

Recognizing your purpose is the first step. Tell your angel what you know about your purpose. Take a few minutes to close your eyes and think about how you feel when you receive this calling or have an awareness about your purpose. Tell your angel about this feeling in your letter.

❖ What you have done about your purpose up to this point? Write a brief summary of actions you have taken to follow your purpose. If your purpose is part of your daily life, include what you are currently doing.

❖ How do you feel when you are in the flow of your purpose? How do you feel when you are not in the flow of your purpose? Where are you now?

❖ What qualities have you discovered in yourself that are the result of following your purpose? How have you benefited from these qualities?

Write a prayer asking to feel the qualities and desires of your soul. Copy the prayer onto a beautiful piece of paper and put it on your altar. Each day, sit at your altar for a few minutes to read the prayer and listen for guidance from your guardian angel. Also, copy the prayer onto an index card and carry it with you, reading it frequently throughout the day.

Watch for hints and opportunities that unfold around this desire and the prayer in your daily life. Write notes as you receive hints, opportunities, and realizations. Take action on them and write about the actions you are taking. Have gratitude for the help you are receiving.

✆ Exercise to Take the Next Step ☙

Taking action on your purpose comes next. On another sheet of paper in your angel journal, make a list of every idea you have received around this calling, no matter how wild or impossible it may seem. Based on this information, write about the following questions:

❖ What are you willing to do to fulfill your purpose?

❖ Would you change your whole way of being for it?

❖ Would you let go of everything you know and go on an adventure into the unknown?

❖ What activities in your life take you toward the fulfillment of your purpose?

❖ What activities take you away?

❖ Can you complete the commitments that take you away from your purpose so you can devote more time, thought, and energy to it?

❖ Can you change your attitude about the way you perform the activities so that they become part of your purpose?

❖ What is missing in your life that has to do with your purpose?

❖ What does your guardian angel want you to know about your purpose?

❖ What does your soul want to do?

❖ What do others need to hear from your soul?

❖ How can you become more responsive to the hints your angel is giving you?

❖ In what areas of your life is there confusion, and what do you need to do to find truth and clarity?

❖ How can you take greater responsibility for the purpose that your soul wants you to fulfill?

❖ What can you do next to more actively follow your purpose?

From the information above, find five action steps you can take toward fulfilling your purpose by making it your life's work. Your life's work may or may not be your job. It could be the attitude with which you do the daily tasks.

Schedule these action steps into your calendar. Write about your feelings as you do them and keep notes about future action steps.

When you don't know what to do next, read through what you have written and again ask your angel to help you find the next step. Next steps can be deceptively simple and obvious. It may seem so simple and obvious that you overlook it and then feel lost. But once you have completed the step in front of you, the next one will appear.

As an example, one day I sat down at my desk to write. Nothing was coming out. As I sat there, I was very bothered that the carpet needed vacuuming, but ignored the feeling. Still nothing was coming, but there was the carpet! Finally about half an hour later, I got out the vacuum and cleaned up around my desk. The moment I put the vacuum cleaner away, I knew what to write next!

ᔪ The Power of Desire ᔫ

Desire is an important key. What do you passionately desire? What are you willing to do to make it happen? Your desire is the force that motivates you to take the necessary actions to fulfill that desire. Desire is also a magnetic force that attracts more of itself to you.

Desire works the same way for both spiritual and material objectives. If you want a new house, that desire motivates you to drive around the neighborhood you want to live in looking for available houses. You take the next step and find a real estate agent who can advise you on what houses are available and connect you with the sellers.

You may have to look at many houses in many different neighborhoods before you find the right one. Desire will keep you from getting discouraged. The first agent may not have the right thing, so you will look for another agent who does. What if you have difficulty qualifying for the loan? You won't give up. You will keep endeavoring until you have succeeded in getting the house you want.

So it is with spiritual desires. If you have the desire to feel the love of God personally, that desire will motivate you to find actions that will attract the presence of God. By taking those actions, your endeavor attracts God's attention. God is waiting to satisfy your desires for His love.

Perhaps you begin by adding more prayer to your life. You may have to try many different ways of praying before you feel a response. If you have enough desire, you won't be discouraged. Your desire will guide you to question what is in the way. What can you do about that? What else can you do? What do you need to learn? Who could help? You won't give up. You will keep endeavoring until you have succeeded in feeling the love that you want.

That love is so rewarding, so satisfying, so enriching that once you have experienced it, nothing else is the same. Your desire increases for more of that love. You find yourself willing to do more, and more, and more, and more until you are firmly situated in God's loving embrace. You have found the faith to leap into His heart.

Your guardian angel is beside you every step of this path: pointing out opportunities; introducing people with similar desires; guiding you to do this, go there, talk to them, open your heart more, take a chance, reach out, let yourself be loved, trust. Your guardian angel helps to keep you focused on finding the next step, then taking that step.

ᔕ Exercise to Find Discernment with Your Desires ᔗ

Miracles happen around the desires of your soul. People show up with just what you need at the perfect moment. Information pops into your mind that you couldn't possibly have known. A check arrives in the mail that is a total surprise in a moment of great need. When things like this are happening, you are in the flow of your purpose.

There are also desires that are not in alignment with your purpose. These desires are connected with negative behaviors and often cause suffering. Perhaps you overeat when you are lonely or anxious. Or, maybe you zone out by watching television rather than thinking about your life.

Write about your desires in your angel journal. Start by making a list of your desires. It may help to think about your desires in the different areas of your life: family and home life, work, relationships, spiritual, financial, physical, recreational, sexual, material, and anything else you can think of.

Look through the list and evaluate which desires are productive and support your purpose. Which desires help you be a better person? Which desires cause you to suffer? Make notes next to the desires.

Highlight the desires that are propelling you toward your purpose. On a separate piece of paper, write each desire that is beneficial, along with a few words on how it connects you to the truer part of yourself. Now use these desires to make an action plan that will help you focus more of your time, energy, and feelings on your purpose in life.

As an example, your purpose may be to provide loving care for dying people. You have a strong desire to become a hospice nurse. Your action plan is to investigate nursing schools and find a part-time job to support yourself while you are in school. To make this possible, you need to reduce your monthly expenses by finding a simple way to live that feels supportive and accurate.

Ask your guardian angel to teach you how to stay focused in your desire as you take each action in your plan to fulfill your purpose. When you are discouraged, turn to your angel for inspiration. Ask your angel for comfort when you are afraid. Seek the qualities of your soul to strengthen and guide you.

✦ Giving ✦

The quality of wanting to give to others comes from the soul. Giving is the natural expression of the soul's desire to share the love that is being received. Giving is also a natural extension of the soul's love for God.

Giving from the heart and the soul is selfless. It is free of judgment and the ego's desire to be recognized. God's love is attracted to those who give with genuine sincerity. The greatest pleasure on the spiritual path is felt through giving to others with no expectation of personal reward.

While you are giving, there is an opportunity to feel yourself as part of the whole. The feeling of being connected is a quality of the soul. The soul is connected to the guardian angels that are helping. In that connection, you are available to receive hints from your guardian angel and are willing to take action. You become God's partner along with your guardian angel.

ᔄ Become God's Partner ᔢ

God is searching for people who want to be His partner in this world. The desire to give to others is one of the qualifications to be in partnership with God. Humility is another qualification. You must be open to His ways in humility so that He can fill you. In partnership with God, He fills you with the qualities of love and the information He wants you to give to others, just as He does with his guardian angels.

The thought of a friend I hadn't talked to in months popped into my mind several days in a row. Finally, I got the hint and called. Gordon was thankful for my call. He had been thinking of me also. As we shared what was happening in our lives, he revealed that he was stuck in fear about speaking to a large group of medical professionals in preparation for a camp for the siblings of children with cancer.

"You love those kids," I reminded him. "You are doing this because you love those kids. The medical people love the kids, too. That is why they are helping. You all know your jobs. Focus on your love for the kids. That's what really matters."

Gordon answered, "I knew that. This call must have been to remind me. I thought I had to figure it all out myself."

You can think of guardian angels as the behind-the-scenes managers for God's will. They know the bigger picture that we don't see. God's will was for the children to receive the love they needed. Gordon's guardian angel knew that he was forgetting the key of love for the children.

Opportunities to give in partnership with God come in an endless multitude of varieties. Some come as hints. I received a hint when I thought of Gordon. Our guardian angels tried to get us together for several days, but we weren't paying attention. Finally I got the hint and made the phone call. Success.

My partnership with God began when I called Gordon and was willing to speak up about love. Gordon entered the partnership when he was willing to let go of being stuck in fear, let go of his way, and focus on the bigger picture of God's way.

❧ Find Ways to Give ❧

Anne in California wrote me a letter saying, "My sister-in-law recovered from cancer. We sat in her hospital room prior to her surgery and she prayed and chose three beautiful angels (or they chose her) to help her come through…I called her the morning of the operation and played Ave Maria over the phone to her. The doctors were amazed at how well the surgery went. God is good. Thank you."

Miracles can happen when you are willing to open your heart in vulnerability to help another. It can be as simple as asking the question, "Do you pray? Would you like me to pray with you?"

Vicki in Washington wrote to me, "I feel like I've received many miracles in my life and sometimes I forget that angels love to minister. I forget that there is infinite abundance and I don't ask because I feel I've already received my fair share or I'm afraid one more miracle for me is one less for someone else. What a wonderful reminder that there are limitless miracles for all of us for the asking."

Do you want to become a partner with your guardian angel in bringing God's love into this world? If so, how can you open your heart and share love in ways that you normally wouldn't?

Giving comes more naturally to some people than to others. If you are not normally open to recognize opportunities to give, make an action plan for giving. Here are some suggestions:

❖ Tithe to nonprofit organizations that make a difference in this world.

❖ Volunteer.

❖ Serve meals to the homeless.

- Visit people who are confined to nursing homes.

- Be a mentor to a child or someone in need of the gifts you have to offer.

- Take your extra blankets to a battered women's shelter.

- Give your pocket change to a homeless person.

- Bring dinner to a sick friend.

- Do laundry for a friend who is overwhelmed at work.

- Help out elderly neighbors.

There was a story on the Internet about a Masai tribe that gave 14 cows to the people of New York City as a gift of care following the September 11th terrorist attacks. They had heard of the attack on a local radio station, but it didn't register with them until Kimeli Naiyomah, a tribe member who is now a medical student in the United States, returned home for a visit. He had been in New York City when the two jets slammed into the World Trade Center towers.

A freelance reporter working in Nairobi said, "What happened in New York City does not make sense to people who live in traditional huts and have never conceived of a building that touches the sky. You cannot easily describe to them buildings that are so high that people die when they jump off them."

But when they heard from Kimeli what happened that day in Manhattan, they were moved to send the cows as a gesture of solidarity. To the Masai people, a cow is equal in value to a child or a plot of land. To them, it was a very sacred gift. All 14 cows were blessed by tribal elders and presented at the U.S. Embassy. The ceremony was attended by hundreds of Masai people, holding banners that read, "To the people of America, we give these cows to help you."

Look deeply within yourself to find ways to give that are personal and meaningful. Give with no expectation of receiving. Give for the pure joy of giving. Give because you want to, not because you think you should. As you give, you are building your relationship with God and your guardian angel.

Prayer — Carry Me Deep Into the Temple of My Soul

My Lord, sometimes I feel so far away from You!
Carry me deep into the temple of my soul where You reside.
Help me to leave behind the busy thoughts
that keep me from You.
Help me to let go of everything and follow my
desire for Your love.
Let my surrender to Your ways be the guide.
Only Your love matters, my Lord.
Show me the way to the place deep in my soul where
pure love flows.
Lead me to the well of pure truth.
Give me the experiences I need to trust you completely
as Jesus did and let go of my separate existence.
The separation from You is torture to my soul.
Help me find the trust to give you everything that
I may live in Your will.
Do what you must to free me from the bondage
of what is false
and bring me Home to pure truth.
Reveal Yourself Beloved One
that I may know You personally and intimately.
Hold me in Your heart that I may become Your servant,
Your lover, Your companion.
Take me, Beloved.
I am Yours.

CHAPTER 9

Gift #7—Love

"*Love wholly and not partially.*
God does not have parts but is present totally everywhere.
(In the same way,) God does not want only a part of you…
Give all of yourself and God will give you all of Himself."

**—Saint Anthony of Padua, an early follower
of Saint Francis**

⚘ The Role of Guardian Angels in Experiencing God's Love ⚘

Guardian angels play an important role in bringing you a more personal experience of God's love. They are our greatest mentors, as they love us unconditionally the way God does. By following their guidance in prayer and meditation, we can travel deep within to the temple of the soul where the love of God dwells. Once you have been touched personally by God's love, you learn from the supreme example of your angel how to share God's love with others.

As the feelings of your soul open up like a rose blossoming, your guardian angel will fortify you with the courage to feel the full spectrum of love's moods. What is the pain of a broken heart but the longing for love? Looking upon one who is suffering terribly, you can't help but feel compelled to help out of loving compassion. And when swept away in ecstatic union, whose love are you feeling but the Lord's?

Dedicate your life to diving deeper and deeper into love. Beg your guardian angel to take you on the journey into the temple of your soul and teach you to live in its richness. Do everything you can to discover the pleasure of God's love in your own heart. God loves you with a passion that you cannot even imagine, but if you ask Him, he will give you a taste! Why not feast on His magnificence?

ᓚ Saint Francis of Assisi ᓚ

Born in the little town of Assisi, Francesco, meaning "the French man," was named in honor of his father's trade with France. As a wealthy fabric merchant, Peter Bernadone had hopes that his young son would learn his trade and take over the family business.

Francis, however, had no such interest. Rather than study, he preferred to focus on dressing richly and spent copious amounts of money on amusements with his friends. When Francis began giving food and money to any beggar he found, his father was not pleased, but neither did he protest.

Dreaming of glory around the age of 20, Francis went to fight for the pope against the Germans. Outfitted in lavish apparel and fine armor, he rode south on his stallion in the company of a knight of Assisi. Along the way, Francis met an old warrior dressed in grungy armor. Francis was so touched with compassion that he exchanged clothes with him.

ᓚ Called to Purpose ᓚ

Soon after, Francis became quite ill. As he lay in a helpless state, a voice told him to turn back and "to serve the Master rather than a man." Francis obeyed the voice.

Francis faced a spiritual crisis when he returned home. He could no longer tolerate the trivial nature of his life and searched for something worthy of his complete devotion. He spent many hours alone, riding in the country.

On one of these rides, he met a leper whose sores were so horrid that Francis recoiled in disgust. Filled with compassion, Francis jumped down from his horse. Taking the man's outstretched hand, he pressed a gift of money into it and kissed it. The leper had disappeared when Francis looked back, leaving Francis with the overwhelming feeling that Christ had appeared to him in the form of the leper.

This experience filled Francis with fervent desire that drove him to spend long hours praying to learn God's will. He visited hospitals and ministered to the sick in his quest for divine love.

✎ Divine Guidance ✎

Deep in prayer at Saint Damian's, an old ruined church near Assisi, Francis felt the eyes of Jesus on the crucifix gazing at him and heard a voice saying three times, "Francis, go and repair My house, which you see is falling down."

In his sincerity and eagerness to follow the guidance, Francis loaded a horse with fabric from his father's warehouse and sold it along with the horse in a nearby town. Francis presented the money to the priest of Saint Damian's church and asked if he could stay there.

When Peter Bernadone discovered what his son had done, he was furious. He brutally beat Francis and locked him up with his feet shackled. Pica, his mother, set Francis free so he could return to Saint Damian's. Peter angrily followed Francis there and insisted that he either return home or renounce his inheritance and pay for what he had taken. Francis returned the money and added, "The clothes I wear are also his," stripping himself. "Hitherto, I have called Peter Bernadone father…from now on I say only, 'Our Father, who art in Heaven.'"

Peter Bernadone left deeply hurt and angry as the bishop who was mediating this whole scene covered Francis with his own cloak. The bishop admired Francis for his fervor and cried while he gave Francis alms. A gardener's tunic was found and, marking a cross on the shoulder with a piece of chalk, Francis dressed and left.

⤳ Sing Praise ⤲

Beginning a strange new life, Francis roamed the countryside singing God's praises. Francis begged food and worked where he could. Through miserable weather and even when beaten by bandits, Francis praised God. He showed us by example that releasing our deepest emotions to God defuses their power to control us.

He became so intimately connected with the earth through his long hours of deep prayer that he praised every experience, from the sweetness of sunrise when the earth awakens to dazzling sunsets and the depths of night.

When Francis returned to Saint Damian's two years later, the priest welcomed him as he began the job of repairing the church. Next, Francis labored to repair an old chapel dedicated to Saint Peter. Impressed with his enthusiasm, many people began to contribute to this work.

Francis was drawn to a tiny chapel in the woods that had been abandoned and was in ruin. Saint Mary of the Portiuncula belonged to a Benedictine monastery on Monte Subasio. In the midst of dreams of living a quiet life as a hermit in this chapel, Francis received a powerful revelation. At the feast of Saint Matthias in 1209, the Gospel of Matthew 10:9–19 pierced Francis, becoming Christ's direct charge to him:

> And going, preach, saying The Kingdom of Heaven is at hand.... Freely you have received, freely give. Take neither gold nor silver nor brass into your purses... nor two coats nor shoes nor a staff.... Behold I send you forth as sheep in the midst of wolves...

Francis removed his shoes and leather belt and threw away his staff. Keeping his woolen coat, he tied it around him with a rope. (This would later become the habit that his Franciscan Friars wore.) The next morning, he began to speak to all he met on the shortness of life, the need of repentance, and the love of God.

People began to seek his warmth, simplicity, and sincerity. Within a year, 12 brothers formed the core of this budding ministry. While working in fields for food and sleeping in barns, Francis wrote the first rule that consisted of some passages from the Gospel and instructions to work hard and live in simplicity and poverty.

Francis took the rules to Rome, requesting papal approval for their new order. While based on Christ's own command, the cardinals thought the rules were impractical. As the matter was being considered, the pope dreamed he saw Francis propping up the Lateran Church with his shoulder. Summoning Francis and his companions, the pope approved their mission and Francis was elected leader. The little band was welcomed to monastic life through the sacred rite of having the crowns of their heads shaved.

✎ The Franciscan Friars ❧

Back in Assisi with papal approval, the crowds were growing when Francis and his brothers spoke. Saint Mary's chapel was offered to Francis, but he would accept only the use of the property. To this day, the Franciscans of Portiuncula send a basket of fish caught in the river each year to the Benedictines of Saint Peter's, and the Benedictines send a barrel of oil to the friars.

The friars built several huts of wood and clay near the chapel and planted a hedge around them. This became their first Franciscan monastery.

Seven hundred years later, people from all religions revere Saint Francis for his compassion and love. So how did he come to acquire such richness within while living in abject poverty?

From youth, Francis was free-spirited and subject to extremes. The passions of his heart guided him into long hours of prayer and meditation in chapels, in caves, and on mountainsides. Francis became intimately connected with the earth during these times, resulting in many miraculous stories with animals.

✎ Give Everything ✎

More important, Francis's relentless desire was rewarded with the personal love of God. The profound beginning of Jesus' gaze from the crucifix at Saint Damian's had meant more than to rebuild that chapel. Francis had been called to rebuild Christendom. God was willing to fill Francis with love because Francis willingly gave everything he received.

Two years before his death, Francis had another powerful visitation from Jesus. Saint Bonaventure described Francis's state when he arrived at La Verna for a time of solitary prayer.

> His unquenchable fire of love for the good Jesus was fanned into such a blaze of flames that many waters could not quench so powerful a love. While Francis was praying on the mountainside, he saw a Seraph with six fiery and shining wings descend from the height of heaven. And when in swift flight the Seraph had reached a spot in the air near the man of God, there appeared between the wings the figure of a man crucified, with his hand and feet

extended in the form of a cross and fastened to the cross. Two of the wings were lifted above his head, two were extended for flight and two covered his whole body.

When Francis saw this, he was overwhelmed and his heart was flooded with a mixture of joy and sorrow. He rejoiced because of the gracious way Christ looked upon him under the appearance of a Seraph, but the fact that he was fastened to a cross pierced his soul with a sword of compassionate sorrow.

—Saint Bonaventure, as quoted in *The Life of Saint Francis*

When the vision ended, Francis was left with a "marvelous ardor" in his heart and markings of the stigmata on his body. Seraphim are the angels closest to God. Burning with love, they bow before the Lord singing, "Holy, holy, holy." The Seraph held Christ in the flaming intensity of God's love. When Francis looked in Jesus's eyes, his heart was pierced with this intensity of love and his body was imprinted with the wounds of the crucifixion.

Francis experienced the unimaginable love of God who holds nothing back, not even the life of His son. Jesus's example of giving so completely that he gave even his body, his blood, and his life for those he loved became the standard of poverty. To Francis, poverty was the blessed result of handing everything over to God or his neighbor in his effort to imitate the limitless love of God.

✎ Letter to Ask Your Angel to Find More Satisfying Love ✎

This deeply satisfying love is to be found in meditation and prayer through an intensely personal and intimate endeavor on your part. Your guardian angel is your guide and knows the path into God's heart well.

Trust your angel and follow where you are led. Each journey offers unique experiences of healing and renewal. The reward is well worth your endeavor. Don't you want to feel the passion of God's desire for you?

Begin by devoting at least 30 minutes to prayer and meditation so that you can drop as deeply into your soul's desire as possible. Then let your heart speak. Write a prayer of your desire to your guardian angel or to God.

Here is a superb example of such a prayer, inspired by Saint Francis and written by a Franciscan priest, Jack Wintz:

> *God of love,*
> *Lead us to the wild, solitary spot in our hearts*
> *where we may encounter your gift of fiery love*
> *and see the gracious way you look upon us*
> *from the cross.*
> *Help us to open ourselves to your limitless love*
> *which holds nothing back from us.*
> *May our hearts catch some of the seraphic flame*

that marked Francis' all-out response to your
great love.
Amen.
—Jack Wintz, in *Lights: Revelations of God's*
Goodness

After you have written your prayer, continue to pray and meditate for another 30 minutes, searching for the response to your desire. Don't stop until you experience some kind of a response from your guardian angel. It is possible for you to have powerful, mystical experiences as Saint Francis did. Or, you may feel a gentle peacefulness.

Have gratitude for the response you receive, whatever it may be. If you are left with an unsatisfied longing, consider that to be a real benediction. You are feeling your soul's desire.

At the end of your meditation, write a second prayer of desire based on what you receive. Copy that prayer onto beautiful paper and place it on your altar. Each day, spend some time at your altar, reading this prayer and searching for a response.

Could you feel your guardian angel guiding you step-by-step? Write about your experience in your angel journal. Describe feelings. List thoughts. Capture realizations. If you had a vision or mystical experience, record every detail you remember so that you can read it over many times for encouragement.

Be alert during your day for responses to your desire. Driving to work, you may suddenly burst into tears of joy for no reason, or be moved to help someone you would have walked past. Watch for opportunities to share the love you are finding with others. Freely and completely, give what you are receiving in gratitude.

✧ From Loneliness to Love ✧

What is your heart crying out for? What is your soul's deepest desire? To find greater love in your life, begin by looking at your current situation. Are you alone after a divorce or the death of your mate? Are you in a relationship with no love? Have you moved to a new city and have no friends? Are you housebound from an illness or injury? Are you a mother with little children to care for and very little adult companionship? Do you feel lonely?

At first, it may seem that loneliness is about other people. But the first relationship to examine is with yourself. What are you feeling? Honestly look at the fears and feelings that are keeping you trapped in loneliness.

After my husband died, I was very lonely and terrified to love another man. What if he died, too? That possibility left me devastated beyond my ability to recover. As I prayed and worked through the fear of loving again, I had to face the fact that everyone I know will die, including me.

There was a big change when I was willing to accept the inevitable pain of loss that accompanied opening my heart to love. I found myself praying for my heart to break open so I could find real love with people. God answered my prayer. As my heart broke open, His love for me gushed in, and I no longer felt lonely.

Soon after, I was able to return to work, teaching workshops for the first time in the four years following my husband's death. As I planned this first trip, I felt tender and wanted to have emotional support from a member of my spiritual community, so I arranged to stay with Dana, who lived in the area. He was standing in the street, eager to welcome me when I drove up.

We didn't know each other, so as the days passed we spent time sharing about our lives. As we talked about mutual friends and experiences we had in common, the level of intimacy I felt with him surprised me. I found myself sharing a depth of truth from my heart that was unusual. By the time I left to return home, we had begun a profound and intimate relationship.

God answered my prayers with Dana. As the relationship continues to grow, we are finding a simple, open honesty with each other that is deeply satisfying. It brings me remarkable pleasure to give to Dana because he receives so thoroughly. Together, we are learning to give as much of ourselves as possible without holding back anything, as Saint Francis did.

After such a long period of suffering, I find myself coming alive in passion with a tenderness that makes it safe and not frightening. At the same time, there is a soberness underlying my feelings because I know that this love is only a temporary gift from God, and I am grateful for every moment.

◌ Exercise to Find Greater Love ◌

I didn't think I could survive another devastating loss. That fear kept me from love. What is it for you? The following questions will help you recognize what you are receiving, look more closely at your desires, and discover where you are blocked so you can find greater love. Write about these questions in your angel journal:

❖ How have you experienced the love of God?

❖ Have you had a taste of love that is without fear, neediness, and jealousy?

❖ How can you have greater intimacy with God, yourself, and your family?

❖ How do you cut yourself off from receiving love?

❖ What fears keep you from loving others?

❖ What old dreams are you clinging to that are in the way of real love?

❖ What old fear and pain do you attach to the people closest to you and how does it prevent you from having more intimacy?

❖ What are you blaming on others that is keeping you distant?

- ❖ What distracts you from your pursuit of God's love?
- ❖ What are you holding back that you aren't willing to give?
- ❖ How can you find the trust to give more?
- ❖ Do you have self-judgments that prevent you from being loved by others?
- ❖ How can you become more alert for opportunities to give?

Be honest with yourself. From this information, make an action plan to find greater love. Begin with your desires. What do you want? Then look at the circumstances and your feelings that appear to be preventing you from having your desire.

Ask your guardian angel to help you make an action plan to increase your experience of love. Find at least five action steps you can take toward your desire.

An action step may be to have a heart-to-heart talk with your mate about what you want. Or perhaps you need to find a new perspective on your current situation. Another action step may be to pray for 30 minutes every morning to let go of a fear that is keeping you from love. Maybe an action step is about finding ways to meet people, or to give. What if you spent a whole day in prayer?

Be specific about your action steps. Write them in your angel journal and schedule them in your calendar. As you take each step, write about what you find as a result and what is next. This will help you to stay focused on your desire, what you are receiving, and where you need to continue focusing. At every step, find ways to include your guardian angel.

On Love

When love beckons to you, follow him,
Though his ways are hard and steep.
And when his wings enfold you, yield to him,
Though the sword hidden among his pinions
may wound you.
And when he speaks to you, believe in him,
Though his voice may shatter your dreams
As the north wind lays waste the garden.

For even as love crowns you so shall he crucify you.
Even as he is for your growth so is he for your pruning.
Even as he ascends to your height and caresses your
tenderest branches that quiver in the sun,
So shall he descend to your roots and shake them
in their clinging to the earth.

Like sheaves of corn he gathers you into himself.
He threshes you to make you naked.
He sifts you to free you from your husks.
He grinds you to whiteness.
He kneads you until you are pliant;
And then he assigns you to his sacred fire,
that you may become sacred bread for God's sacred feast.

All these things shall love do unto you
that you may know the secrets of your heart,
And in that knowledge become a fragment of Life's heart.

But if in your fear, you would see only love's peace
and love's pleasure,
Then it is better for you that you cover your nakedness
and pass out of love's threshing floor,
Into the seasonless world where you shall laugh,
but not all of your laughter,
and weep, but not all of your tears.

Love gives naught but itself and takes naught but itself.
Love possesses not nor would it be possessed;
For love is sufficient unto love.

When you love you should not say,
"God is in my heart," but rather,
"I am in the heart of God."
And think not you can direct the course of love, for love,
If it finds you worthy, directs your course.

Love has no other desire but to fulfill itself.
But if you love and must needs have desires,
let these be your desires:
To melt and be like a running brook that
sings its melody to the night.
To know the pain of too much tenderness.
To be wounded by your own understanding of love;
And to bleed willingly and joyfully.
To wake at dawn with a winged heart
and give thanks for another day of loving;
To rest at noon hour and meditate love's ecstasy;
To return home at eventide with gratitude.
And then to sleep with a prayer for the
beloved in your heart
and a song of praise upon your lips.

—Kahlil Gibran, Lebanese-born American poet, mystic,
and painter, from *The Prophet*

CHAPTER 10

Angel-Guided Prayer and Meditation

"Therefore I tell you, whatever you ask in prayer,
believe that you receive it, and you will."

—Mark 11:24

✧ The Temple of the Soul ✧

The purpose of prayer and meditation is to take you to a place deep enough within your self where you can attract the presence of the Lord. Your guardian angel is your guide on this journey within. The place you are going is the temple of the soul.

The temple of the soul is a feeling and a state of consciousness. It is the truest part of your being and is connected with your soul. It is here that you experience and begin to develop the qualities of your soul.

You find this place during prayer and meditation. The temple of the soul is found beneath your surface feelings. Your angel will guide you on a journey through your emotions and thoughts that are causing disturbance. As each feeling and thought comes into your awareness, you are guided to find healing or acceptance so you can let go.

In this way, you peel away layer after layer of baggage from your past as well as current feelings, looking for the stillness that is beneath the agitation. Your soul lies waiting with your purpose in that stillness. The Lord is also waiting there to shower you with more love than can be imagine as you get a taste of the vastness of eternity.

Once inside the temple of the soul, many qualities await your discovery and exploration. Love, trust, devotion, humility, gratitude, longing, surrender, courage, and truth are just a few of the qualities of your soul. As you feel each quality, you are carried far beyond what your mind could have imagined. You are saturated with a wealth of experiences and permeated by treasures of realizations. Touching this place changes you forever.

Now you can bring the treasures of realizations and experiences into your life. Be patient with yourself. Keep searching until you succeed in finding the way into the temple of the soul.

ᕣ Prayer ᕤ

Prayer is a very personal and powerful way to have conversations with God. Speak to God as if He is your best friend because He is. Tell Him your deepest desires. It is difficult to imagine the love that awaits you when God touches your heart. Let Mother Frances Cabrini inspire you with her prayer of passionate love and surrender:

Oh, Jesus, I love You so much, so much!
I am being consumed by Your love…
but notwithstanding such intense ardor,
I see, I feel that it is only a pale shadow
compared to the fire of love with which
You surround me.
Give me a heart as large as the Universe so that I
may love You…
Oh, Adorable Heart of Jesus, most loving Heart, …

Love, what do You wish me to do? ... Do with me as You will.”

—As quoted in Timothy Conway, Ph.D., *Women of Power and Grace*

In your prayer, pour your heart out in a plea for help. Speak of the devotion and desire you feel in your soul. If you are alone, speak out loud. Praying out loud in humility increases the power of your prayer. Hearing your own words can help you to feel them more intensely.

Feeling true humility in your heart is a link to the loving assistance of your guardian angel. In humility, you are open to receive the help you are asking for. In humility, you are willing to follow God's will. In humility, you recognize that His will is what your soul desperately desires. In humility, you can feel your love for God.

☙ Pray Believing ❧

Try an experiment. Just believe. Jesus said to pray believing. Have faith. Act as if you have trust. Listen for the desires of God. Watch for His answers to your requests. Watch for the ways He guides you. Be open to possibilities. Look for opportunities and take action upon them.

If you don't currently pray and don't know where to start, ask your guardian angel to help you find your personal relationship with God through prayer. Start with what you are feeling. Don't have judgments about any feelings.

Find the place of willingness in your heart to share everything with God. Then He can help you.

Ask your guardian angel to help you with a prayer like this one:

> *Guardian angel, please help me.*
> *I don't know God. I am afraid of His greatness.*
> *Does He even hear my prayers?*
> *He has never answered them before.*
> *I don't think He listens to me.*
> *Please, help me to open my heart and pray so that*
> *God can hear me. Please help me find the depth*
> *of prayer from my soul that God can answer.*
> *Help me to pray believing and to recognize*
> *His response.*

Exposing painful feelings and doubts in prayer with a desire to let go of them opens space for God to touch your heart with His love. He is waiting for you to reach out to Him. Pray believing that the Lord is listening. He is. He hears every prayer.

⤳ The Power of Prayer ⤶

I had an experience that opened my eyes to the power of prayer as I traveled on September 13, 2001, right after terrorists crashed hijacked planes in New York, Maryland, and Washington, D.C.

Boarding a small plane in Central America, I passed an incubator that held a tiny premature infant no larger than my hand. A nurse carefully attended the child in its minute-by-minute fight for life. Already traumatized by the terrorist events, this infant made me especially aware of the frailty of life.

Midway through the flight, a woman from the back of the plane moved to a seat near me. Shortly after that, a man followed and sat behind her. Suddenly, he started shouting cruel and obscene accusations at her and then beat her back and head with his fist. At the same time, he was pawing at the emergency exit door she was sitting next to, as if he wanted to open it and push her out.

I was horrified. I had never witnessed such violence. The woman looked at me and mouthed the words, "Help me!" Frozen with fear, I was unable to think what to do and stared back with a shocked, blank face.

"PRAY!" screamed in my head, breaking the frozen feeling, and I began the most intense prayer of my life for help. The only words I could think of were, "My God, please intercede! Help us now." Instantly, the violent man became quiet. The woman moved to the back of the plane near the infant and asked the male passengers to help.

Three passengers moved up to surround the abusive man. One sat behind the man, poised in the seat with his belt wrapped around his hands, as if ready to strangle the abusive man. I was overwhelmed by the feelings of rage and self-righteous retribution coming from the men who were trying to help.

It suddenly occurred to me that if a fight broke out, they would all end up in my lap! I quickly moved to the back of the plane and continued to pray with urgency and intensity. My life depended upon this prayer: "Lord, please! Let your influence be more powerful than anger and violence."

The most amazing thing happened. The abusive man passed out. There was nothing for the other men to do. No fight. For the remaining 45 minutes of the flight, the men sat poised, as if hoping for a fight, while I prayed desperately for the abusive man to stay asleep. He didn't wake up until after we had landed and gotten off the plane.

I was deeply grateful that my guardian angel screamed the word "Pray!" into my thoughts and led me step-by-step through this horrifying experience. It made me vividly aware of how swiftly and powerfully God can intercede in direct response to the intensity of prayer. I will never again underestimate the power of prayer.

✆ Forms of Prayer ✆

There is no prayer that God does not hear. The prayers that come from your soul's desire connect you directly with His heart. Ask your guardian angel to help you find your soul's desire.

Start where you are. Feel yourself. Feel your desires, pain, and longing. The energy of your feelings opens your heart so you can feel God respond. Love is a feeling. If you heart is closed and you are unwilling to feel, love cannot enter you.

Sincerity is also a feeling. No matter what condition you find yourself in, pray to God with honesty and sincerity. Ask your guardian angel to help you honestly expose your situation. Have a sincere desire to know the truth. Trust that God is hearing your prayer, and stay open to receive His response in whatever forms it comes. Your desire makes it happen.

Let the circumstances of your life offer the triggers to open your heart to deep prayer. For instance, when your heart is broken in a relationship, cry. Cry a river of tears when you feel the deep sorrow and grief of the separation from loved ones who are dying or leaving you. Find comfort in the arms of your guardian angel as you let your broken heart cry to God for His love, compassion, and healing.

Perhaps you will ask your guardian angel for help with a problem. You may experience the response from God as focused determination while you search for truth by sitting in deep, silent prayer.

You may feel rage that shakes you to your foundation because of the unfair things that happen on this earth. Let that rage become your plea to find compassion.

Being touched by the grace of God can bring tears of gratitude streaming down your face. Or, your guardian angel may whirl you around in a dance of ecstasy as you feel the joy of knowing your Beloved. It may also be natural for you to give yourself to God in devotion and love.

Plan prayer time into your life. Can you sit in your bed and pray for 15 minutes every morning before getting up? Do you pray in the shower? While driving to work? During exercise? While you fold laundry? Can you devote 30 minutes to prayer before bed?

How can you make ordinary tasks more meaningful with prayer? How much time can you find to devote fully to God? Make a plan. Put it into your schedule and follow your plan.

꩜ Answers to Prayer ꩜

As you develop your relationship with your guardian angel, be open to receive while you give. It is easy to overlook the many tiny ways that prayers are answered. When you haven't noticed the results, you may become discouraged and stop trying.

Your guardian angel is infinitely creative in responding to prayer, so be alert as you watch for these influences. Make an effort to notice the smallest changes. Focus on gratitude that you are finding a connection with your guardian angel.

Feeling an increased desire to connect with God is an answer to prayer. So is experiencing greater trust. Having the courage to pray directly to God if you haven't before is an answer to prayer. Finding more clarity about the subject of your prayer is a direct response. Being able to feel the pain in your heart that you usually ignore is also a benefit of prayer.

Feeling different at the end of the prayer than you did at the beginning is a wonderful result. Did you feel more peace, gratitude, openness, or love? Was there an increased sense of devotion? Did you receive a rush of energy and the strength to face your challenges?

Did you receive some new information? Has something happened in your life to present an opportunity? Did someone you know offer an answer to the question you were praying about?

Feeling gratitude and appreciation for what your guardian angel is giving you. God wants to give you so much!

⤳ Go to Sleep in Prayer ⤿

The time spent in deep sleep can be used for rapid spiritual movement. While sleeping, the judgments and beliefs that are a part of your waking consciousness sleep with you. These judgments and beliefs control the way you experience life and color the insight, information, and inspiration you receive when awake.

While the body sleeps, your soul is awake and open to receive guidance in a way that is not possible while your conscious mind is operating. Use this precious time by simply going to sleep in prayer.

Each night before sleep, create a short and specific prayer asking for what you need. Ask for help with life circumstances, information about something, or a request for deeper union with God. As you go to sleep, focus your attention on your prayer in an open and receptive state. Repeat it over and over until you are asleep.

As you are saying your prayer, focus on your desire to feel a direct experience of God's presence. This may be feelings of peace, calm, love, or trust. Let go of any expectations that you feel a certain way. That is your conscious mind interfering with a preference. You may feel agitated and unable to sleep. It may seem like a current of electricity is flowing through you. You may feel fearful. God's personal touch comes in infinite forms. When you wake during the night, repeat your prayer until you fall asleep again.

First thing in the morning, take the time to remember what happened during the night. Did your dreams contain inspiration or information you need? Did you wake up knowing something new? Did you have a realization?

Write your prayers and experiences down in your angel journal. Thank your guardian angel.

Prayer to Let Go to the Lord

Father of Everything, thank you for holding this child so close to You.
I thought I was lost, but when I opened my heart to look for You—there You were!

*When I turned my attention off myself and onto
You, You filled me with love.*

*When I asked what You wanted, the answers came
into my mind.*

When I followed Your ways,

*You flooded me with ecstasy and the energy to do as
You asked.*

*When I asked for help, the saints marched in with
joy beaming from their eyes.*

*My Lord, as I give to You, I receive back so much
more!*

Thank you for holding me so closely.

*Experiences like this dispel my fear and help me to
fall into Your arms in trust.*

*Thank you for giving me everything I need to come
closer to You.*

*While I sleep, help me to find complete trust in Your
ways and Your love that I may finally let go of my
existence to You.*

❧ Meditation ❧

Meditation is your endeavor to connect with the presence
of God. There are many different forms of meditation.
Some, like prayer, are intended to help you become calm
and still. Many of us have such strong emotions bottled
up inside that sitting still and trying to be calm is impos-

ible. When that is the case, more dynamic forms of medation help you to move through disturbing thoughts and feelings so you can release them and open your heart.

Once your heart is open, you can easily drop into the temple of the soul and God's presence. In this place you find deep states of calm that are surprisingly intense and a depth of love that is awesome. Here you find the qualities of your soul and the information about your purpose that will lead to a more fulfilling life and more satisfying relationships. Your guardian angel is your guide on these adventures within.

❧ Prepare for Meditation ❧

Music can help you find the way into your heart through your feelings. The following soundtracks are perfect for this form of dynamic prayer and meditation. The music on the following albums flows through many different moods to help you open and express these feelings within yourself:

Passion, Peter Gabriel

Braveheart, James Horner

The Mission, Ennio Morricone

Gladiator, Hans Zimmer and Lisa Gerrard

The Last of the Mohicans, Trevor Jones and Randy Edelman

1492 Conquest of Paradise, Vangelis

Once you have acquired some supportive music, prepar
an area for meditation. Have a stereo or boom box set u
to play music. Arrange the CDs or cassettes you hav
selected so they are easily accessible and won't b
a distraction.

You may want to create an altar in the room where you
will meditate. It could be your angel altar, or a second
altar. Ask your guardian angel to guide you in creating
this altar so you can find the trust to surrender to deep
prayer and meditation.

Give yourself some room to get up and move around
Clear away any objects that you might bump into or trip
over. Have a box of tissues, a towel, a pillow, and you
angel journal. Tell housemates that you need some privacy
and are going to make noise. Assure them that you are
okay and not to be worried or distressed by what they
may hear. Invite them to join you!

✎ How to Meditate ✎

When you are ready to begin, select a length of time for
your meditation, such as 45 minutes or two hours. Ask
your guardian angel to help you open your heart and take
you to the temple of your soul so you can feel God's love

Notice what you are feeling. Feelings or thoughts triggered from your day may be waiting for you. Start with
them. Select music that matches your feelings. For example, if you are angry or agitated, select intense music. I

you are joyful, play music that enhances that feeling. See the following sections on moods to help you understand how to select music.

Let your feelings move with the music. Expressing emotion moves your feelings. Then be open and receptive to experience what comes up next. If you don't have strong feelings to start with, begin sitting up and search within. You may find a quiet place and fall silently into it, dropping deeper and deeper.

Your guardian angel is your guide during meditation. Many different feelings will be introduced for your attention. As each thought and feeling comes up, your angel is inviting you to clear it out so you can be free of it. It's like peeling the layers of an onion as you cry your way through. As each layer is peeled away, your angel is guiding you deeper toward the temple of your soul where God's love is waiting.

Trust your angel. You can move through painful emotions quickly and find remarkable healing by following your angel's guidance. It's simple. Give your full focus to what you are feeling or thinking with the desire to face it, feel it, and let it go completely.

Pray as you go. Talk to your angel or to God about what you are feeling and about your desires. Keep looking for the next feeling and the next old issue. Following are suggestions for moving through specific feelings.

✎ Devotion and Depth ✎

You may find that your angel has guided you to a state of quiet devotion and depth. Music can help to enhance the sensation of falling deeper inside yourself. This is the feeling of connecting with your soul, your guardian angel, and God. Sit with a still body and plunge deeper and deeper within.

Supportive music:

Passion, Peter Gabriel: "Open," "With This Love"

Gladiator, Hans Zimmer and Lisa Gerrard: "Elysium," "Honor Him," "Now We Are Free"

Baraka, L. Subramaniam: "Wandering Saint"

Devi, Chloe Goodchild: "Thy Will/Jaya Bhagavan," "Ave Maria"

Music to Disappear In, Raphael: "In Paradiso," "Resurrection"

A German Requiem, Op. 45, Brahms: First movement

✎ Sadness and Longing ✎

Are you so lonely that your heart bleeds for love? Have you lost someone in the breakup of a relationship? Do you feel a longing for something; you don't even know what? Are you sad or in despair about the suffering of those you love or your own life? Has someone you love died?

Your guardian angel is extending healing for your broken heart. Cry. Let the tears flow. Let the feelings come out that you have been holding for so long. Curl up into a little ball like a child and cry into a pillow. Beg your guardian angel to hold you and comfort you. Cry with the prayer to open your heart to God's love. He is waiting inside the pain to hold you.

Muffle your crying sounds in a towel or a pillow so you don't disturb others. You may be afraid to start crying because it seems like you won't be able to stop, or you may already have cried an ocean of tears that didn't seem to help. To have a change of heart, you must cry with the desire to let go of your pain and find something new. Let your guardian angel guide you. Having a prayer of desire to change is vital. Here is an example:

> *Dear guardian angel, I am so afraid to feel the pain!*
> *Please give me the courage to stop holding myself*
> *together and let my heart break.*
> *Please help me to let go of the ways I hang*
> *onto my pain.*
> *Please help me find the desire to let*
> *God's love heal me.*

Supportive music:

> *The Mission*, Ennio Morricone: "On Earth as It Is in Heaven"
>
> *Braveheart*, James Horner: "For the Love of a Princess"

The Last of the Mohicans, Trevor Jones and Randy Edelman: "Cora"

Passion, Peter Gabriel: "With This Love"

Daydream, Mariah Carey: "One Sweet Day," and "Open Arms"

Celine Dion, Celine Dion: "My Heart Will Go On"

Palestrina Missa Papae Marcelli, Allegri: "Miserere"

The Mirror Pool, Lisa Gerrard: "Sanvean"

ᴥ Agitation and Anger ᴥ

During meditation, when you feel unbearable agitation inside, scream. Your guardian angel is guiding you into a place where powerful transformation and healing can occur.

When feeling anger or rage, take your guardian angel's hand and scream! Let these feelings out in the safety of your prayer with a desire to release the pain and find more love. Take responsibility for yourself and scream into a towel or a pillow to muffle the sound, so your family and neighbors are not disturbed and worried about you.

Screaming uses the force and energy of the anger or agitation to break apart the position you are hanging on to. To accomplish this, scream with your mouth closed, one hand holding the towel firmly over your mouth, and the other hand holding the towel firmly around your vocal chords. Direct the energy of the scream down into your belly, not out like catharsis.

Screaming, with the desire to let go of your feelings and to change, opens more space inside for you to receive the personal presence and energy of God's love. With His help, you can change.

Call to your angel to help you release your anger with the desire to let go and find a deeper feeling of truth. Expressing the energy of your feelings from the position of being right is self-righteousness. You must find the willingness in yourself to let go of your attachment to being entitled to your feelings of anger or agitation.

Beg your angel:

> *Please show me the way to let go of these feelings*
> *of anger and agitation. Please help me to find*
> *the truth.*

Anger and agitation are powerful forces for change. Your willingness to change combined with this intense energy of anger breaks up concepts about how you should be, how your world should be, how others should treat you, how God is. It breaks up defensiveness.

Let yourself feel the consequences of anger. What does it do to you? How does it make you treat others? How does it affect the ones you love? How do you treat yourself when you are angry? Allow yourself to break open from the intensity of your feelings until you are devastated and vulnerable. In that openness, you will find truth and healing.

The energy in anger and frustration can be transformed into passion for change. Together with your prayer, they have the power to break through old habits that you have been unsuccessful in changing. What do you want to change into? That is an important question. Always strive for truth and greater awareness.

The objective is to release the emotional charge so you can find a calm place in yourself. From that calm, you can think clearly and find the truth in the situation. Speak to others and make choices from truth and clarity rather than anger and agitation.

Let the feeling of desire burn in you. Desire to be free from the ways you make yourself suffer. Desire to have a greater experience of God's personal love for you. Desire to know your true being in God. Desire to know God's will for you.

Supportive music:

1492 Conquest of Paradise, Vangelis: "Light and Shadow," "Conquest of Paradise," "Hispanola"

Passion, Peter Gabriel: "The Feeling Begins," "Of These—Hope," "A Different Drum," "Passion"

The Last of the Mohicans, Trevor Jones and Randy Edelman: "Elk Hunt," "Fort Battle," "Massacre/Canoes"

Braveheart, James Horner: "Battle of Stirling," "Betrayal & Desolation"

Jars of Clay, Jars of Clay: "Worlds Apart," "Sinking," "Liquid"

Ozzmosis, Ozzy Osbourne: "I Just Want You," "Denial"

Abraxis Pool, Abraxas Pool: "Don't Give Up"

Edge of the Century, Styx: :"Show Me the Way"

Rattle and Hum, U2: "Desire," "I Still Haven't Found What I'm Looking For," "Pride (In the Name of Love)"

✎ Move, Dance, and Celebrate ✍

Your guardian angel may inspire you to move! When you feel the desire to move, do what you are imagining rather than watch. Let your body dance with the music. It may want to move in ways that surprise you. Let go of concepts that you should sit still or move in a certain way! Allow your body to move the way it wants to move. Let yourself feel the freedom of moving your body and your feelings. Move with a prayer to be filled with the presence of God.

> *Oh my Lord!*
> *Fill me more!*
> *Take me more!*
> *I am Yours!*

The feeling to move may have many different emotional qualities. It could be joyous and ecstatic celebration, it could have a sensuous feeling, or it may have a feeling of intense determination. Select music that supports the feeling as you dance with your guardian angel.

Be responsible for your movements. Don't do anything that will cause injury to yourself or anyone else.

Supportive music:

> *Simply the Best*, Tina Turner: "The Best"
>
> *Fly*, Sarah Brightman: "Heaven Is Here," "You Take My Breath Away"
>
> *Martika's Kitchen*, Martika: "Love…Thy Will Be Done"
>
> *Pointer Sisters Greatest Hits*, Pointer Sisters: "Jump (For My Love)," "Freedom"
>
> *Savage Garden*, Savage Garden: "Truly Madly Deeply"
>
> *Sun Machine*, Dario G.: "Sunchyme"
>
> *GHV2*, Madonna: "Deeper and Deeper," "Ray of Light"

✍ Calm and Think at the End of Meditation ✍

Take a few minutes at the end of each meditation to calm and find balance before you go back into the world. This is especially important when your meditation was intense or deep. Sit up for five to 15 minutes and find a calm feeling within.

Finish the meditation by thinking. Write about the questions that apply to your experience in your angel journal:

- ❖ What did you experience?
- ❖ What painful feelings did you move through?
- ❖ Was something healed?
- ❖ Did you experience qualities of your soul?
- ❖ Did you feel the temple of your soul?
- ❖ Were you touched by God's love?
- ❖ How did you feel your guardian angel guiding you?
- ❖ Did you receive information about your purpose?
- ❖ What realizations did you have?
- ❖ Did you receive information?
- ❖ Did you find actions to take?

Each meditation is a success no matter how it may have seemed. Just the fact that you meditated made it successful. Giving time to your spiritual advancement, no matter how it may have felt, is more important than you can imagine. The conscious mind is not always aware of what happens in the soul. Trust that your guardian angel took you where you needed to go.

If you feel agitated after an intense experience, focus the energy of the agitation toward your desires. Think of the agitation as passion and put it to productive use. Ask your guardian angel to show you how. Find courage and try again!

The Earth Braces Itself

The earth braces itself for the feet
Of a lover of God about to
Dance.

The sky becomes very timid
When a great saint starts waving his arms
In joy,

For the sky knows its prized fixtures,
The sun, moon, and planets
Could all wind up
Rolling so wild on the floor!

My dear, this world, its laws,
Are such a minute part of existence.

Should not all of our suffering and sadness
Be like this:

As just dropped from an infant's palm
That is asleep against the breast
Of God?

The earth braces itself for the feet of Hafiz.
The sky pulls a mirror from its pocket
And is practicing looking
Coy,

For the Beloved has at last
Opened His arms
And is inviting my heart to eternally
Dance!
The day candle (sun) has forgotten the hour:
The whole world has gone joyously mad.

Look,
The Sun's sweet cheeks are blushing
In the middle of the night

Desiring the rampage of the feet
Of God's lovers.

—Hafiz, Sufi poet of Persia (1320–1389), in *The Gift*,
translated by Daniel Ladinsky

CHAPTER 11

Angel-Inspired Shrines and Altars

"It isn't necessary that we stay in church in order to remain in God's presence. We can make our heart a chapel where we can go anytime to talk to God privately. These conversations can be so loving and gentle, and anyone can have them. So why not begin?
He may be waiting for us to take the first step."

—Brother Lawrence, a French Carmelite monk (1611–1691), in *The Practice of the Presence of God*

৵ **Personal Sacred Space** ৵

An altar or a shrine is a personal sacred place you create in your home. Invite your guardian angel to guide you in creating an altar or shrine. In this way, the altar will be infused with the presence of your guardian angel and can become your meeting place.

Go to your altar or shrine to be with your guardian angel. It is a personal place to pray and to listen. You are inviting a more intimate relationship with your guardian angel by creating an altar or shrine in your home, and then using it regularly.

Devotion is a quality of your soul. Ask your guardian angel to help you experience feelings of devotion as you co-create your altar, then continue to develop this important quality by caring for your altar as a way to give to your angel in devotion.

Set aside at least 30 minutes to create your altar or shrine. It is an important start in developing your relationship with your guardian angel. The longer you can give, the greater your chance of being touched by spirit. If you have a family or housemates, consider asking them to join you. Praying and performing acts of devotion together can bring a closeness to your family that little else can achieve.

❧ Feeling Devotion ❧

Start with some music that kindles a feeling of devotion in your heart—not thoughts in your mind, but feelings in your heart. Sit in prayer and listen to the music. Go with what you are feeling. That may be a feeling of still, deep desire. You may be urged to move with the music. Trust your feelings and follow them.

Music suggestions that convey a feeling of devotion:

Devi, Chloe Goodchild

Music to Disappear In, Raphael

The Silent Path, Robert Haig Coxon

Deep Peace, Bill Douglas

City of Angels: "An Angel Falls," "The Unfeeling Kiss," "Spreading Wings," "City of Angels"

Missa de beata Virgine, Giovanni Pierluigi da Palestrina

❧ Locating the Altar ❧

To select the location for your altar, pray about it. With an open heart and mind, ask your guardian angel where to place the altar. Find the words that describe your longing. Your prayer may be something like this:

Guardian angel, please guide me.
Help me find a location for this altar, where

your spirit can be present in my home.
I want to feel a deeper connection with you.
I want to learn your ways.
Let this altar become the place where we can meet.

Be open to receive a response. You may think of a place or get a picture in your mind. You may have a feeling that relates to a location. This is your answer. Trust it. Don't question.

You may get a feeling for a location that is far from home. It could be a place that you have dreamed of going, or a place where you felt deep peace or connection with spirit. If that happens, use the feeling you have for that place to help you find devotion where you are. For now, ask again for a location in your home or garden. You may want to go to that distant place at another time to create an altar.

If you don't notice a feeling or a hint, don't give up and think you aren't getting it. Take a moment to notice if you have a concept about what to feel or get. Let that concept go and find openness. Walk around your home looking at areas until you do get a feeling. The feeling could be a thought that this is a good place. You may find yourself looking at a particular spot. It doesn't have to be an earth-shaking response.

Here are some suggestions:

❖ the mantle of a fireplace

❖ the baby's room

❖ a section of countertop in the kitchen

- ❖ the top of a dresser or table
- ❖ a corner of your desk
- ❖ a little shelf by your bed
- ❖ the top of the toilet tank
- ❖ by the mirror in the bathroom
- ❖ a table in a hall
- ❖ a shelf in your closet
- ❖ an alcove

↫ Creating the Altar ↬

Go to the location you have selected and be open to receive more information. Set a small statue of your guardian angel in place and observe your feelings. Is this the location for this statue? If this is the right location, you may feel a lightness of being, or joy and enthusiasm. You may feel a deep calm or sadness.

Act out what you feel. This is an opportunity to connect with your feelings and find some freedom in doing things you wouldn't ordinarily do. Sing, dance, spin around, or cry. You may experience peace and want to sit in prayer or chant. Be receptive to any feelings or thoughts you have. They are all hints at the direction for you to go.

Start asking questions. Does the angel want a cloth under the statue? It could be a scarf, place mat, tablecloth, or piece of fabric. Do you have a beautiful doily that you grandmother crocheted or embroidered? Could it be part of a veil from a wedding gown? How about something from your daughter's dress-up box? Be creative. Gather what you have and try out each piece one at a time. You will know when you find the one.

Is there a candle for this altar? What kind? A tea light? Votive? Tall? Short? Scented? What color? What kind of holder? Try different possibilities.

Is there a picture that wants to go on this altar? Should the picture be in a frame on the surface or hanging on the wall?

What else? Incense? Flowers? A plant? Perhaps the pebble you found during a profound experience of prayer while walking on the beach. The objects that go on your altar should be articles that are sacred to you. Anything that helps you feel a connection with your guardian angel belongs on this altar. There are no set rules for altars. The altar may want to be very simple with only a few things. Trust your feelings.

ᕫ Bring Your Altar to Life ᕬ

An altar can become a living part of your life. To keep it alive, visit the altar daily. Change the objects often. Freshen the flowers. Burn incense. Light the candle.

Once you have created your first altar, you may feel the desire to make altars everywhere! There are so many forms of God with which to develop a personal relationship! What deity do you want for the next altar? God himself? Jesus? The Mother? Buddha? Goddess? Quan Yin? Kali? Krishna? Your personal spiritual teacher?

Your guardian angel is helping you to feel the ways of God when you connect with the desire to honor the forms of the Lord. You are giving to God when you take the time to create an altar. You are feeling your devotion when you tend to the altar daily. You are succeeding in developing a deeper relationship with God as you find these feelings in yourself.

✋ Your Body as an Altar ✌

Altars can also be built within. The temple of your soul is an altar for the presence of God. Make your heart a meeting place with your guardian angel by listening within so you can hear when your angel brings guidance. Be alert for hints in the events around you as your angel answers prayers.

Your angel lives in loving devotion to God. How would your day be different if you prepared yourself as an act of loving devotion each morning? How would you be different if you took the time to find a connection with God in morning prayer, then dressed to express the quality of love you felt?

> My Lord, how shall I feel in You today?
> What flavor of Your love can I express through
> my appearance and feeling?

There is an endless variety to the qualities of how God's love feels. Your prayer one day may have a soft and sensual feeling with your Beloved, so you wear silky fabrics with soft colors that cling sensually to your body. The next may be powerful and focused, so you choose stark black and white with crisp fabrics to keep you grounded as you move through an intense day. Your prayer may bring you into a deep state of peace, so you select loose-fitting, comfortable clothing to help you continue in the feeling of peace.

Wear an angel pin to help you remember to stay connected with the presence you found in your morning prayer. Be reminded by the pin that your angel is walking with you through the day, and be open to interactions.

◈ Make Your Whole House an Altar ◈

Once you have experienced the benefits of having a sacred space in your home, you may want to expand that space. Welcome your guardian angel into more of your home by working on one area at a time.

It is difficult for your guardian angel to come into an area that is cluttered. Taking action to clean and organize with the intent to open space for your guardian angel is a powerful spiritual practice. Clutter around you is a reflection of clutter in your mind and emotions. Cleaning and organizing an area of clutter in your environment will automatically act to clean and organize areas of your mind and consciousness. You will feel yourself let go of chaos both emotionally and mentally after cleaning house.

How can you make every place in your home have a sacred feeling of devotion? How can you prepare your home so that it invites your guardian angel's presence?

❧ Make a Plan ❧

Ask your angel to walk with you through your home to identify the areas that need attention, and write them down. Pick the area that has the highest priority or that is bothering you the most. Set a time in your schedule to work on it. You may want to make this a regular spiritual practice and devote Saturday mornings for the next month to working on your home.

The objective is to create sacredness that invites your angel's presence, having exactly what you need where you need it, no more and no less. Think about the area you are going to work on. Do you need to shop for any supplies before you start? Does anyone need to help you? The area may have things that belong to other people, or boxes too heavy for you to lift alone. How long do you estimate it will take to clean this area? If you don't finish the first time, when can you schedule more time to complete the job?

❧ The Bedroom Closet ❧

The bedroom closet is a good example for a first project. The goal is to end up with a closet that inspires you to feel the connection with the truer part of yourself and your life's purpose. Ask your guardian angel to help you create sacred closet space.

Remove clothes that don't fit, are worn or damaged, or you don't wear. Be honest. Cut deep. Don't hang on to the dream that you will fit into pants that are too small. Clothes that don't fit are skeletons from the past in your closet. If you don't want to give them away, put them in a box in the garage. Let go of clothes that you paid a fortune for but have never worn. They are ghosts. Take out clothes that are no longer your style. Get rid of colors that don't bring out the best in you. Dowdy, frumpy, out-of-style clothes—out.

Put all your old shoes in a bag and take them away. Save only the shoes that go with the clothing you keep. Do the same with accessories. Put that scarf that you love that doesn't go with anything in a box in the garage. Another ghost.

The objective is to end up with only clothes that you love to wear and the shoes and accessories that go with them. Then it is a pleasure to open the closet to find the right thing. You no longer have to wade through ghosts and skeletons.

Dress yourself so that you feel beautiful or attractive to God. As you work on your clothing, work on your appearance until you love your reflection in the mirror. Find a hairstyle and color that brings out your best features. Women, get your eyebrows waxed. Have a makeover to update your image. Get a manicure and pedicure. Finding the beauty and love in yourself is a spiritual practice of devotion when you do it to please your Beloved.

You may end up with only a few outfits. That makes it simple. Be sure that each outfit is complete. Hang complete outfits together so you can grab one hanger and you have all the parts. Have the hangers and clothes all facing the same direction. Group like colors together or put work clothes on one side and casual clothes on the other.

Think about the kind of clothes you need so that you have clothes for work, exercise, play, and sports. Have just what you need—no more and no less. Consider getting one style and color of hanger if your hangers are an assortment. You will be amazed at the difference in how it feels to have consistency.

Transform your closet into a place of clarity and beauty. Remove objects that you don't actively use, such as boxes of old pictures. Bring consciousness to the things that must remain in your closet.

Take that box of pictures, for example. Go through the pictures. Throw away the pictures that aren't worth saving. Only keep the best ones. Put them into an album or special box so they are organized. You have only what you need. No more and no less. Arrange the box or the album beautifully in the closet with the other things so that when you look at it, there is nothing to do. You feel peaceful. This is what it means to bring consciousness to things.

Keep going in your consciousness. Think about the things you removed. Go through the things so that you keep only what you want and need. What do you want to keep? Where can it go? What can you give to friends and family? What can you give away?

The next part of your action plan is to take these things all the way to completion. Don't stop until you are finished. The off-season clothes are neatly boxed in the garage. You have given your favorite hot pink suit that doesn't feel like you anymore to your friend who loves it. The old clothes have gone to a homeless shelter. The extra family pictures are mailed to your kids. Done. Savor that feeling of completion.

The objective is to have a beautiful closet with everything you need, no more and no less. Do you have a welcoming feeling when you open the doors and look in? Do you love the clothes you have and feel good dressed in them? Take the time to enjoy these qualities.

Can you feel the difference between how your closet was before and how it is after? Can you feel a quality of devotion in the care for your things? Can you feel the quality of simplicity in having everything you need, no more and no less? When you remove distraction, you open space for your angel to interact with you and help you dress for your soul's purpose.

Now that you have felt the benefits of bringing consciousness to the first area, look at your list of areas that remain. Which one bothers you the most? Approach your whole house in the same way as the bedroom closet.

Make time in your schedule. Think ahead. Do you need to buy any supplies for the project? Do you need to coordinate with anyone to help you?

The Linen Closet

Is the linen closet your next project? Again, the goal is to end up with a sacred space that inspires you to feel the connection with the truer part of yourself and your life's purpose. Ask your guardian angel to help.

Go through your linens. If you have a monster pile of sheets, look at each sheet. What kind of condition is it in? Would you really want to sleep on it? Does it have matching parts—bottom and top sheets and pillowcases? How many extra sets do you really need? If you have lots of company, put together complete sets that are in the best condition and fit the beds that you have available for guests. Put all the leftovers in a pile.

What about pillows? How many extra pillows do you have? How many do you need? Pick the best ones and put the others in the leftover pile. Now for the blankets. Which blankets fit the beds you have? How many blankets do you need to go with the sheets you are keeping? Make sure you have what you need. No more and no less.

Towel time. Look at your towels. If you have a big pile, select the towels that match your colors and are in the best condition. Again think about how many you would need for guests. Keep towels for the beach or pool. Don't forget the dog towel—if you have a dog—and set aside cleaning rags. Put the rest in the leftover pile.

What else is in your linen closet? Take everything out and look at it. Do you use it? Do you need it? Does it belong in this closet? If you use it and it doesn't belong in this closet, where should it be? If it is stuff that you have somehow ended up with, never use, and don't really want, put it in the leftover pile.

We all end up with so much stuff we don't really want but don't know what to do with. Give it away! That's what you do with it. You don't have to save presents that you don't like. Let go of old family stuff that is just junk. You don't have to keep it.

Now it's time to organize. Neatly fold each of the pieces that you are keeping. Fold the towels the same way so that when you stack them they are an even size, with the fold facing you. Do the same with the sheets and blankets.

Put everything back into the closet the way you would see it in a store. Arrange the things by type, color, and size and in an order that makes sense when you need something. For example, if you have two colors of towels for different bathrooms, put them in two piles side-by-side if you have the room. That makes it simple to put the towels away and get them when needed. Put the twin bed sheets and blankets together in one place, next to the king sheets and blankets.

The objective is to end up with a beautiful linen closet that brings you pleasure when you open the door. Each item is folded neatly and in its place. What about that extra stuff that needs to be in here? Bring consciousness to the objects the way you did in your bedroom closet.

Camera gear is a good example. You may have several different kinds of cameras: a video recorder, a digital camera, and a regular camera. Each camera has film, batteries, bags, straps, flashes, and lenses. Go through the accessories. What do you really need and use? What is extra? Put the extras you never use onto the leftover pile.

Think about how to organize the pieces you need. If each camera has a bag, perhaps you want to pack each bag neatly with its camera, attachments, extra batteries, and film. If you don't use camera bags, would a bin work? Do you want a separate bin for each camera with its attachments, batteries, and film? Maybe a little drawer unit that fits in your larger closet would be even better? Have each camera ready to use when you finish so you can just grab it off the shelf and shoot.

Under ideal circumstances, arrange your linen closet to look like store shelves when finished. Is each item complete and presented in a functional and beautiful way? Were you able to match the bins and drawers or use color coding?

Do you have a label maker? Consider labeling the shelves to make it easier for family and household members to return items to the right place. For example: Downstairs bathroom towels. Blue towels. Twin beds. Guest bed. Winter blankets. Cameras. Be creative while keeping it simple and obvious.

Now look at the leftover pile. Is there anything that a family member or friend would want? Call them to ask if they want it. Get some bags and put the items for specific people in a bag. Write their names on the bags. When can you take it to them? Are they coming over for dinner? Put the bags in the right place for this transfer. Is that in the car ready to deliver, or by the door waiting for a pickup?

Where could the other stuff go? The Salvation Army? Does your church take these things for charity or rummage sales? Take the time to beautifully fold the leftovers and neatly bag or box them for the charity. Schedule time to drop them off. Put the bags or boxes in the best place for this transfer. Be completely finished. Don't leave any part of the task dangling.

Here's the best part. View your handiwork. Take the time to let yourself really feel the difference between beautiful and well organized with just what you need, and such a mess that you don't even want to open the closet door. You will feel a difference—even when your things were pretty neat (but you still had to dig through stuff to find what you need). What a relief to open the closet and easily see what you need! Simple. Open. Complete. Give yourself this gift.

You will be surprised at how much more open and receptive you are to the assistance of your guardian angel when your home is clean and well organized. Perhaps you want to put a reminder of your guardian angel in the closet by taping a meaningful picture to the inside of the closet door. Then each time you open the closet, you can have a moment with your angel.

❧ The Kitchen ❧

Once you have felt the victory and joy of having your bedroom and linen closets beautiful and well organized, are you ready to tackle the kitchen? Transform your kitchen to a sacred space where your angel would want to cook with you!

Open each drawer and cupboard one at a time, and look at the things you have. Do you use them? If not, start a leftover pile. The objective is to end up with the cookware and kitchen supplies that you need. No more and no less.

Take the silverware drawer, for example. Do you have three different sets of silverware jammed into the drawer? Which set do you prefer to use? Do you find yourself pawing through the other silverware on top to find the kind you like? Do the other sets of silverware need to be in this drawer? Do you ever use them? Maybe you like to use one set for guests. Could the extra set be in a separate silverware tray somewhere else for when guests come? Is some of the silverware extra and not needed? Wrap it in a bag and put it into the leftover pile.

In the pots and pans cupboard, are there pans you don't use? Take them out. How could you arrange the pans to be more efficient? Do you have a giant stack of baking pans and sheets that you never use? Take them out. Keep a cookie sheet for Christmas, just in case.

Under the kitchen sink, what do you use? Are there bottles of products that you don't use? Throw them out. If you are a saver, it can be very therapeutic to throw stuff away.

Like the linen closet, the objective in the kitchen is to end up with everything you need and no more. Simple and easy to find. No molding food in the refrigerator. The right set of mixing bowls. You don't have to dig through 50 spice bottles to find the basil.

Do you dare to move on to the garage? You have the idea by now. As you clear out each area of your home, prepare it so that your guardian angel would feel welcome. Make each area an altar of devotion. Take the time to appreciate the difference in how each area feels after you have organized it. Let that feeling be the incentive to keep it this way. Schedule time to refresh each area weekly.

225

Prayer to Let Go of Toys

Guardian angel,
I feel like a child in a playroom, surrounded
by too many toys.
This child has gotten older and no longer feels a
fascination with any of the toys.
Too old for toys and don't know what is next.
Just sitting here, surrounded by all these dead toys,
feeling uncomfortable and anxious.
Yes, that's me.
Chaos, overwhelming complexity, and endless
tasks were my toys.
Thank God, I have outgrown them.
The parts still clutter my room and lay in waste
around me waiting to be cleaned up.
One by one, I put them away.
In the trash, out of my consciousness, away, away.
Slowly, the room is becoming organized.
Simple.
Free of clutter.
Free of excess.
Simple.
Angel, I don't know how to be simple.

Teach me your ways.
Help me to feel what is old, heavy, no longer useful, and
weighing me down.
I want to feel light and free for you.
Help me to let go of my old ways of clinging to things
for fear that I won't have enough.
Those things have become heavy and pull me away from
your outstretched hand.
Like a drowning person holding onto a heavy bag,
unable to reach the rescuer's hand.
Let go.
Reach to the Lord for Freedom!
Simply let go.
Trust God.
Simple.

CHAPTER 12

A Walk with Your Angel

God sent us an angel and brought us out of Egypt.

—Numbers 20:16

๑ Walk with Your Guardian Angel ๑

One way to have a deeper relationship is to invite your guardian angel to walk with you. Walking with your angel should be an inspirational time, filled with healing and regeneration. As you walk, talk with your angel in a very personal and intimate way.

Expressing your feelings honestly helps you to open up and release excessive emotions so you can become calm and clear. Be bold and direct. When situations in life are troubling you, share them with your guardian angel and ask for help. Then be open and listen for a response.

Answers to the problems you are addressing in this kind of prayerful exchange with your angel become more apparent when you are in an open and receptive state. On the days when your heart is filled with love and gratitude and the details of life are far from your mind, share these golden moments your angel as well.

This is a time to investigate your relationship with your guardian angel and to look more deeply into yourself. You may also use this time to talk about your desires, consider decisions you need to make, and plan your next steps with the guidance of your angel.

The key focus for the walk is your desire and willingness to be changed. To be changed means to let go of your current position and find something new about the situation. For example, if you are upset, you can be changed by the willingness to seek solutions rather than continuing to justify why you are upset. Likewise, if you have been clinging to a picture of how you want something to be, focus on your desire to find other possibilities. And when you have a judgment about a person or situation, strive to see the situation from their perspective.

You must have the desire to change in order for your angel to help you. This willingness creates a receptive state in which you can quickly let go of anger and pain and have great experiences of love. With an open mind, you can receive new information to solve problems or see situations from a different perspective.

God sent the angels to help us with the difficulties of life, so we can find the joy of experiencing His personal love. Walking in prayer with the desire to have a direct experience with your angel brings you closer to God. Each time you let go of pain to find more love, you have succeeded at touching God's heart.

Before you embark on such an inspirational journey with your angel, prepare by selecting the topic you need help with. Plan where you will walk and when. Prepare to enter into communion with your angel, who is your best friend and the helpmate God has given you with devotion and appreciation.

✎ How to Pick a Topic for a Prayer Walk with Your Angel ✐

The best topic for a prayer walk with your angel is the most urgent situation in your life that you want to address.

This topic could be about a decision you need to make or a desire you have for a change. If you are in conflict with someone, the topic could be about finding resolution.

Following are examples of situations to help you identify the specific topics you may want to address. Maybe you don't like your job and have been thinking about finding a different occupation. Or perhaps you often feel lonely and want more intimate friendships.

Are financial problems troubling you? Do you need to return to work after being out of the job market for a number of years? Is your child having difficulty in school and you don't know what to do?

Are you in conflict with someone? Is your family situation changing? Have you had a painful argument with someone you care about? Do you disagree with a co-worker?

What are your desires? Perhaps you have been feeling the desire to live somewhere else. Or maybe you feel the longing for more love?

≪ Questions to Contemplate ≫

After selecting the topic, search for several questions that will help you discover the core of the dilemma. Here are some examples of the kinds of questions that are helpful. They come from a wide range of topics, so select the ones that pertain to your topic. Make notes in your angel journal as you prepare for your walk.

- ❖ What are you afraid of?
- ❖ Are you frustrated at not being able to find a solution to a persistent problem?
- ❖ Do you feel stuck in a situation and don't know which direction to take?
- ❖ What doubts do you have about your guardian angel caring for you personally?
- ❖ Have you done something that made you feel ashamed or embarrassed?
- ❖ Are you overwhelmed with the pain of losing someone you love?
- ❖ Are you feeling joyous and grateful for the blessings in your life?
- ❖ Do you simply love God and want to express your feelings?
- ❖ What matters most to you?
- ❖ What don't you like about your life and want to change?
- ❖ What do you want from a relationship with your angel?
- ❖ What is the purpose of your life?
- ❖ What are the qualities of your soul?
- ❖ What gifts have you received from God?
- ❖ What actions can you take to find a deeper connection with your angel?
- ❖ How can you have more trust in God's ways?

✎ Exercise to Help You Determine Your Own Prayer Walk Topic ✎

Before you begin your walk, sit for ten minutes in a quiet place and reflect on your life using the questions just listed. Do not try to answer all the questions at this point

Make a list in the back of your angel journal of your personal situations that you want your angel to help with Update this list regularly by removing topics that are complete and adding new ones. Refer to this list before each walk. Select one topic that is most urgent for your walk. Write that topic on the next regular page of your journal.

It is critical to identify the questions that are specific to the area in which you need help. Finding precise and relevant questions about your topic opens the door for you to receive the help you need on your walk with your angel.

For example, it may feel as if everything is most urgent. If that's the case, perhaps the feeling of being overwhelmed is the topic of your walk. On the next regular page in your journal write your topic, "The feeling of being overwhelmed by everything I have to do."

Next, brainstorm for questions pertaining to this feeling that will help you find the core essence of the situation and write them in your journal:

❖ What is causing this feeling of being overwhelmed?

❖ What payoff do you get from being continuously overwhelmed?

- ❖ Does it make you feel important and needed?
- ❖ How do you perpetuate feeling overwhelmed by never finishing anything?
- ❖ What tasks could you finish quickly and easily to get the feeling of completion?
- ❖ Is time management an issue?

The point of this exercise is to help you find the key questions you will contemplate with your guardian angel. Don't answer the questions now. Write the topic and these key questions on the note pad you will take with you on the walk to help you stay focused.

✺ How to Walk—The Preferred Gait for Walking Meditation ✺

The purpose of the walk is to open your emotions while praying for a change of heart. Your angel is by your side to encourage and support this opening. The feeling of your prayer will determine the speed and intensity of your walk.

If your prayer is calm and deeply focused within, you may walk slowly and deliberately. When your prayer is joyful, you may walk with a rapid, light spring in your step. During feelings of anger, resentment, or frustration, walk at a speed and intensity that matches your emotions.

For example, if you just had a fight with your spouse and are very angry, it is the perfect time for a prayer walk. Walk fast, hard, and with determination to release intense feelings of anger, resentment, or frustration. Let your arms swing as you pump out these feelings. With every step, have the intention to blow off this steam. At the beginning of the walk, speak honestly about your feelings in prayer with your angel. Be graphic and specific as you talk with your angel about the situation. Let the fur fly as you get it out.

While you express your feelings, have the intention to let go of anger and find openness for a new solution. At some point, the intensity of your anger will lessen and it may even feel emptied out. Your walk will naturally slow down as you begin to calm. This is the time to pray for the desire to change if you aren't beginning to feel it.

As you calm, think about the situation with a willingness to receive new information. Ask your angel for help. Listen for answers. At this point, you may be walking very slowly as you become more focused within. Allow your walk to be a natural expression of your feelings.

✺ How to Prepare for Your Walk ✺

Before you go out for your walk, think about the conditions and prepare yourself accordingly. As an example, I like to walk around my neighborhood each morning for about 30 minutes to find my focus and connection with God for the day. I wear comfortable running shoes and ress for the weather. In a fanny pack, I take tissues and a small note pad and pencil to make notes when I receive information or inspiration. I also take a small bottle of water, lip balm, and a house key.

Plan ahead before you go out. Wear comfortable clothes that you can move in. How long will you walk? If the sun is out, do you need to wear sunscreen? Will you need a hat and sunglasses? What kind of shoes will give you the comfort and support you need for the terrain where you will be walking? Do you need to wear a watch so you will be on time for your next commitment? How much water will you drink? Should you take a sweater or jacket? Are you staying out long enough to need a snack?

If you don't have pockets, you may want to wear a fanny pack. Carry identification and a little money. Take tissues and a small notebook and pencil to take notes. Do you want to wear an angel pin to help keep you focused on the purpose for your walk?

If it's windy, do you need earplugs or a scarf so you don't get an earache? If your angel were your mom, how would she dress you so you felt lovingly cared for? Is there snow out? You can prayer-walk with your angel wearing snow-shoes or cross-country skis.

I love to hike alone with God on remote mountain trails. The feeling of exhilaration from the mountain air and the influence of silence open me to profound experiences. When I do this, I tell someone where I am going and when I expect to return. I always take basic emergency supplies in my fanny pack when I hike.

In addition to the standard identification, tissues, not pad, and pencil, these supplies include three protein bars bug repellant, a space blanket and rain poncho that bot fold up small and flat, a short length of rope, strong clot tape with the tube taken out and pressed flat, a pocket knife, bandages of various sizes, Neosporin, several anti septic wipes, a lighter, a small flat mirror that could b used to signal for help, a sandwich-size Ziploc bag, an water. I wear a small flashlight and whistle on a cor around my neck along with a bandana. I tie a wind breaker or light jacket around my waist and always wea a hat.

I have been surprised by how many of these supplies have used. Many times, I've been able to share the feelin of care by cleaning and bandaging a cut for someone came across on the trail. Once my little dog fell into mud bog. I rinsed her off in a stream and carried he wrapped in the bandana until she warmed up and recov ered from the shock. Another time, I cut som beautiful flowers to give to a friend with the pocketknif and carried them back in the Ziploc bag. I have use the bag to carry trash out. Several times, I have com across swarms of insects and was relieved to have th bug repellant.

As you gather the supplies you will take, prepare yoursel to be in communion with your angel. Begin searching fo the topic for your prayer. Make up a simple blessing i which you thank God for the gift of your angel who i walking with you through life. Perhaps you need to fin a quality within yourself such as peace or gratitude. As your angel to help you find this needed quality.

⤐ Where to Walk ⤏

Find a place to walk that is convenient and easily accessible, such as the streets of your neighborhood. Perhaps there is a large park close by with walking trails. It is easier to concentrate on your prayer and conversation if the path you are walking on is relatively flat and not too crowded. Finding your way through mobs of people is too distracting. Crowded boardwalks at the beach in the middle of summer or busy sidewalks downtown are not good places. Pick safe locations and times to walk where you won't be in danger from human or animal predators.

Select a terrain that is suitable for your level of health. Walking on sand when you have hip or knee problems is not wise. If the path is too steep, your attention will be on the next step rather than prayer.

It is easier to feel the influence of the angels in the beauty of nature. I'm fortunate enough to live by the ocean. When time permits, I love to take long prayer walks on the beach with my angel. The feeling of openness from the vast spaces, purity from the fresh air and blue water, and the warmth of sunshine on my face make it easy to let go of tension and feel God's love.

The solitude of mountain trails welcomes deep communion as you feel the presence of angelic beings in the trees and in delightfully sweet fragrances. Babbling brooks pour through the soul, washing you clean. God's wisdom is more easily heard in this silence.

One spring, I spent a month in the mountains and hiked three to five hours every day. The purpose of the hikes was to find a deeper, more personal relationship with God. I sang to God as I hiked each day, pouring out my love, talking about concerns and decisions I needed to make, letting go of painful feelings, and finding my way through loneliness. As I sang, God responded by filling me with more love than I could have ever imagined and providing surprising information and answers to persistent problems.

Over the month as I built strength and acclimated to the altitude, I made several long and steep climbs that resulted in powerful prayers and experiences of great joy. By the end of the month, I was flooded in God's personal love for me.

∽ When and How Long to Walk ∾

It is ideal to set up a regular time and place to walk, so that it becomes natural and easy. You are more likely to walk when you don't have to think much about how to prepare, where to go, or how to get there. The time and length of the walk you select depends on your schedule and needs.

Walking daily for 15 to 60 minutes helps you develop a rhythm and feeling of devotion in your prayer. As you become more comfortable with walking in prayer and seeking a connection with your angel, it gets easier to find deeper desires and more honesty. Each time you pray with an open heart and mind, you discover more about yourself, your angel, and God. Your angel becomes more easily accessible as she gets to know you and tunes in to the schedule.

I like to walk for 30 minutes each morning to connect with my angel and prepare for the day. A daily walk during a lunch break can be powerful as you let go of what happened during the morning and refocus for the afternoon. Perhaps later in the morning after the kids have gone to school is sweet time alone with your angel and the Lord. Or you may need to walk with your child in a stroller, inviting both your angels to be there.

After work, at sunset, or at the end of your day can be an important time to review what happened and receive the guidance of your angel in making a plan for the next day. Walking in the moonlight is a sacred, peaceful energy that can engender great receptivity to the influence of your angel.

In addition to regular prayer walks, go when you are overwhelmed with emotion. For example, at the beginning of a disagreement with your spouse, stop and go for a walk. Use the walk to release anger, then ask your angel to help you find a solution to the problem. Return when you can listen calmly and speak from truth rather than out of anger.

Prayer-walk when you are stuck on something. When I am working on a problem and don't feel like I'm making progress, I often go for a prayer walk and pray about it. I admit that I don't know what to do and ask for help. Then I search for the part of myself that wants to find a solution. Invariably, I receive a little tidbit of information or a change in my feelings and I am able to find the next step.

You don't need to walk the entire time. You can sit as needed. If you are in poor health or recovering from an injury, don't let that stop you. Set it up so you can be successful. You may have "prayer sits" where a friend takes you to a bench in a beautiful place and you sit with your angel. If you are confined to a wheelchair, find a way to make it work.

Longer walks of three or more hours are very beneficial when taken weekly. You have more time to focus on specific life problems or to contemplate spiritual questions. Several hours of concentrated prayer allows your heart and mind to open deeply enough to receive profound personal experiences with the angels.

Give yourself the gift of taking several long prayer walks on consecutive days. For example, on a holiday weekend devote three hours each day to prayerful hiking in a beautiful place in nature. You will be amazed by the abundance of gifts God wants to shower on you. He is just waiting for you to want Him and be open to receive His love. It may take some determination on your part to break through fear or doubt you may have before He can reach you. It is worth it.

✑ How to Commune with Your Guardian Angel while You Walk ✐

Imagine that your best friend is walking by your side and you are having a conversation. You feel comfortable sharing your deepest, most personal feelings. You have great respect for this friend and trust the wisdom shared with you. You feel profound gratitude for the love and intimacy you feel in this relationship.

Your soul already lives in this connection with your angel. Some days, you may be able to tap directly into that feeling and be renewed by its richness. Other days, you may not feel anything and need to face the doubt, fears, and issues that are covering over this connection.

Prayer is a personal conversation with spirit. By what name will you address your best friend? Talk to your friend about your feelings and desires with honesty and directness. If no one is around, speak out loud. I often sing using a simple melody.

Begin with the topic you selected. Focus on one thing rather than jumping around to complain about all the problems in your life. Describe the topic just as you would when talking with a friend. Make the description specific and detailed so that you are very clear about it. Ask yourself questions to find even more clarity.

Let yourself feel the consequences of this topic. As if you were talking to your trusted friend, express how you feel. Using the example of being in debt, tell your friend how frustrated you feel because you are not making progress.

Expose feeling ashamed of your financial position. Lament about how it affects your family. List the ways you feel trapped, stuck, or victimized by the circumstance. Explore the many feelings related to this issue.

Next, find the willingness in yourself to change and recognize new solutions that you have never seen before. That means letting go of the reasons and excuses you have for why you are stuck in this situation. This is a vital key. Your guardian angel cannot help you if you are unwilling to change.

Finally, listen for answers. Be aware of shifts in your emotions and thoughts. Let solutions come to you. When you receive an idea or thought, write it on your note pad. At the moment, it may seem like a very strong idea that you won't forget. Write it down anyway. Or it may seem like something very simple that you should have known all along, but didn't notice. Write it down. You may receive ideas or thoughts that seem unrelated. Write them down. Perhaps you find yourself speaking a very specific prayer for this topic that you want to write down and continue to use.

∽ Recognize Evidence of Communion with Your Guardian Angel ∾

Many barely noticeable shifts can happen as a result of connecting with your angel. Be alert and notice everything. Feeling different at the end of the walk is evidence that you have made a connection with your angel.

Perhaps you started the walk agitated about your topic and by the end you feel calmer. Maybe you felt lonely at the beginning and had a sense of companionship by the end.

The range of experience can be huge. Did a rush of ecstatic energy sweep you away? Were you filled with joy or bubbling over with enthusiasm? Did you suddenly burst into laughter for no reason? Sometimes, powerful realizations pop in and you understand something that has been a mystery. Perhaps you dropped into a state of peace.

Receiving information that you didn't have at the beginning is powerful evidence of your connection with your best friend, your angel. You may know the next step to take. Clear answers may have come to you. Did a friend pop into your mind that you could ask for help? This kind of information is often very simple and clear. You may be tempted to overlook it because it is so simple and may seem as if you already knew it. You may receive an outpouring of information and need to sit to write it down.

Did you feel the presence of your friend? It may have seemed as if someone was there with you. You may have felt a tingling sensation. Sometimes it feels like your hand is being held or your cheek brushed. Do you feel more loved?

Write down feelings, changes, realizations, thoughts, and ideas you notice along the walk in your notebook. No matter how insignificant they may seem, write them down. These little bits of evidence that you have had a connection with your angel can help you to build trust that this relationship is real.

When you return home, write in your journal about your experience and what you received. On days when you cannot feel a response, read your notes and find comfort.

After the walk, continue to look for responses to your prayer. Several hours later, you may realize how to resolve a problem. Maybe the friend who came to mind during the walk calls with a bit of information that you needed. You might have a synchronistic meeting while in line at the bank when an old acquaintance comes in with information about a job that would be more enjoyable and pay more than the one you have now. Add these events to your journal notes to fortify your trust that your guardian angel is listening and responding to your prayers.

✍ How to Avoid Distraction and Stay Focused ✍

Any number of things can happen during a walk. Sometimes the line between distraction and answer to your prayer can be thin, so use awareness. Friends are the biggest outer distraction. Before your friend decides to join you, clearly explain the purpose of the walk and tell the friend you will be silent. It is not a social occasion. Don't try to match walking paces. Before you start, talk about the need to walk at different speeds and be totally focused on your topic. Perhaps you start out together and set up a time and place to meet at the end.

During the walk itself, you may come face-to-face with a stranger or a friend and have the feeling you need to speak with them. Follow your feeling. Keep the conversation short and try to quickly determine if this meeting is a distraction or has a purpose related to your prayer. It may be enough to get a name and phone number, continue your walk, and then call the person later. This person may have the information you need or know someone who does.

Someone may need your help. Stop and give it to them if it feels like the thing to do. When that happens, God is calling on you to be His partner in caring for one of His children. That person's guardian angel may be requesting your human support. Use careful discretion so that you don't jeopardize your physical safety.

If your prayer or thoughts are deep and focused, you may feel like walking with your head down to avoid eye contact with people. You may be bursting with joy and want to make eye contact with everyone! Trust your feelings while staying focused on being with your angel in prayer and contemplation of your topic. There is no right or wrong way to do this.

Your mind is the biggest source of inner distraction. It may not want to focus on your topic and try to wander all over. Gently bring it back to the topic. You may need to do this every two seconds and feel quite frustrated. When that happens, your topic has just become training the mind to stay focused. Let your frustration build and be a force for change. Ask for help from your angel. Walk fast and with intensity. Let your steps and breathing help you to continuously bring your focus back to the topic.

Turn your frustration into a prayer for help. Rather than beat yourself up with questions like, "Why can't I stay focused?" pray, "Dear angel, please teach me how to stay focused on you." It may be necessary to repeat that prayer over and over until you can regain control of your mind. Battles like this will result in greater control over your thoughts.

Each time you are distracted, talk with your angel about it. Ask for help. Return to your topic. Prayer is a very personal thing. Don't try to compare your prayers to those you have read or heard. Let them flow naturally from your heart and soul.

The following is a prayer I sang to my Lord on a walk. It is simple and direct. Each line is an expression of what I was feeling in that moment. I was changed by the end of this prayer. You can have immediate responses, too. An open heart and mind are a welcome invitation to your angel and the Lord.

Prayer of Gratitude

Thank you, Father,
I feel so loved.
So cared for.
Thank you for bursting through the wall of
loneliness and despair
with Your loving touch.
Thank you for showing me how much
You love me through
the words of the people in my life.
Thank you for providing everything I need to
come closer to You.
Thank you for the humility that I feel as this
help comes to me.
Thank you for reminding me that I am not
apart from You.
I feel so loved.
So cared for.
Thank you for stripping me bare so that I can learn
to care for others as You care for me.
Thank you for alleviating my fears.
You know my heart better than I do.
Thank you, Father, for the benediction of Your
active participation
in this humble life.

CHAPTER 13

Action Plans

"*Your soul learns which activities bring
God's presence nearer.
It remains in His presence by practicing those activities.*"

—Brother Lawrence, a French Carmelite Monk
(1611–1691), in *The Practice of the Presence of God*

✧ **How to Make an Action Plan** ✧

An action plan is the set of steps needed to accomplish a task. Think of it as an organizational system. The task may be something material, like organizing a closet. It could be emotional, such as dealing with feelings from the breakup of a relationship. Perhaps it is a mental task, where you need to think clearly to make an important choice. Or the task could have a spiritual goal, such as wanting to feel the love of God.

In each of the "Gift" chapters, you were guided through making specific action plans. Draw upon those experiences now to encourage you to make a life practice of using action plans.

Begin by gathering your angel journal and a pen or pencil, and then sit in prayer. Ask your guardian angel to help you find clarity and truth. Then examine the task you need to focus on by answering the following questions in your angel journal. Not all questions may apply to your task. Focus on the ones that do:

❖ Clearly identify the question, problem, or project.

❖ How does this apply to your life's purpose?

❖ Does this have you trapped in some way? How? What does the trap look like?

❖ What do you need? Does it involve other people? Do you need supplies?

❖ When can you schedule time to work on this project?

- ❖ Think about each step you need to take and the order in which to take them.

- ❖ Do you need more information? Where can you find this information?

- ❖ Do you need help from someone else?

- ❖ What do you need to change in yourself? What actions can you take to make that change?

- ❖ What action steps do you need to take? In what order?

- ❖ Write a prayer to keep your focus on taking positive action.

After you have prayed, thought about the task, and found some actions to take, copy the actions onto some kind of sign that will help you stay focused on the course of action you have chosen. One possibility is to copy the actions onto an index card and carry it with you so you can read it frequently during the day, specifically when the issue or question comes up.

I like to type my action plans in big letters and tape them to the wall over my desk where I will look at them all day as I work. The bathroom mirror is a great place for action plans that have to do with self-judgments and attitudes about your appearance.

Another suggestion is to draw your action plan in big letters on a piece of paper and stick it to the wall by your bed. A friend was having difficulty getting situated in a new town after moving across country. Finding a new job and feeling at home were quite a challenge emotionally and mentally.

She made six signs with the steps for her action plan and taped them to a screen next to her bed. In that position, they were very visible and supportive as she made phone calls in her job search. A few of her action steps were:

❖ Nothing is wrong with me.

❖ One moment at a time.

❖ Pray, pray, pray.

ও Daily Spiritual Programs ৯

A daily program consists of the specific activities that will help you advance spiritually. Begin by thinking about what you want to accomplish. What obstacles are in the way? Which practices will help you? Which practices call to you and you feel eager to begin?

Be specific about your program and write it into your schedule. Design your program to meet your personal needs. Here is an example of how to apply what you have learned in these chapters to your life:

❖ At night before bed, write in your angel journal about your spiritual desires, prayers, what happened during the day in relation to those desires, what actions you took, and the realizations you had.

❖ Write a prayer to help you get through something

or to take you into a deeper connection of love with God. Go to sleep in that prayer.

- ❖ In the morning, sit up for ten minutes and reflect on what happened during the night in response to your prayer. Make some notes in your journal.

- ❖ Meditate and pray. Take 30 minutes to release your feelings that are stirred up by the events of life. Ask your angel to use those triggers to guide you into deeper feelings of desire for God's love. Calm your emotions and make an action plan of specific steps you can take to come closer to your desire.

- ❖ Go to work. Before you begin your work, say a prayer asking your guardian angel to help you. Periodically during the day, remember your angel and God.

- ❖ Use transition times to pray and to feel the comfort of your angel. Pray while you walk to the bathroom. Pray as you stand in line at the bank. Open your heart to the Lord before you make a phone call with a prayer that the other person will be able to feel your sincere desire to be helpful.

- ❖ After work, go on a prayer walk with your angel to move through the feelings of the day and have some time with your Beloved.

- ❖ On Saturday, go to a retirement or nursing home and be with someone who is lonely. Open your heart to them. Let yourself feel their pain. Listen. Give them your attention and care. Love them.

❖ Spend time contemplating a behavior that is counterproductive. Ask your guardian angel for help. Look at it from different angles. See how it affects people you care about and keeps you distant from them. Pray about it. What triggers it? How does it control how you respond? Are there related behaviors? Meditate to expose the feelings behind it and release the emotional charge. Think about actions you can take to change. Take the actions and change.

❖ Regularly get together with a group of friends with a common interest of spiritual movement. Pick a topic to learn about and discuss. You may belong to a group. Open your heart to these friends so that you can find honest, intimate, loving, and satisfying relationships. Share yourself.

Use your daily spiritual program to focus on your life's purpose. Choose actions and practices that will move you closer to fulfilling that purpose. William James was a psychologist and philosopher from Harvard around the turn of the century. He said, "Knowledge about life is one thing; effective occupation of a place in life, with its dynamic currents passing through your being, is another."

The Holy Spirit is a tangible energy that can be felt. When you are connected with your soul's purpose, guided by your guardian angel and actively taking each step that is put before you, this dynamic current of spirit can be felt as it passes through you.

You may not know more about your purpose than your next step. But as you take it, you will feel that current of energy sustaining you as the next step after it appears. Have faith. You are being guided by your guardian angel to fulfill your purpose. Do as much as you can and the Lord will see that you are rewarded.

Prayer to Give My Life
to the Lord

Guardian angel,
Please help me to give my life to the Lord.
I need you to hold my hand every step I take.
Open my eyes that I may see the opportunities you bring.
Help me to find my desire to know God.
Teach me to pray from my soul so that God can
feel my desire for Him.
Take my fears and doubts that stop me from
believing that He is there.
Draw my attention to the behaviors that prevent me
from feeling His love.
Help me to find the courage to crumble
as I let go of these old ways of being.
Show me how to meditate so that triggered feelings
can be the catalyst to
crack my heart open to the love of God.
My Lord, I need you now!
I want to find sincere desire within myself!
Expose the selfishness that I hide in.

I want to feel true loving care for other people.
Take away the ways I pretend.
Strip me down so I can have honest, intimate,
satisfying relationships.
This depth can only be found in my soul's connection
with God.
Please, show me the way.
Please, help to give my life to the Lord.

Resources

Saint Theresa of Lisieux. *The Autobiography of Saint Theresa of Lisieux*. John Beeres, Translator. New York, NY: Image Books by Doubleday, 1957.

Brother Lawrence. *The Practice of the Presence of God*. Springdale, PA: Whitaker House, 1982.

Carson, C., and K. Shepard (Eds.). *A Call to Conscience, The Landmark Speeches of Dr. Martin Luther King Jr.* New York, NY: Warner Books, Inc., 2001.

Conway, Timothy, Ph.D. *Women of Power and Grace*. Santa Barbara, CA: The Wake Up Press, 1994.

Cristiani, Msgr. Leon. *Saint Joan of Arc*. Boston, MA: Daughters of St. Paul, 1977.

Desmond, Edward. "Pencil in the Hand of God" *Time*, December 4, 1989.

Gibran, Kahlil. *The Prophet*. New York, NY: Random House, 1976.

Hafiz, Daniel Ladinsky (Trans.). *The Gift*. New York, NY: Penguin Putnam Inc., 1999.

Hanh, Thich Nhat. *Living Buddha, Living Christ*. New York, NY: Riverhead Books, a division of Penguin Putman Inc., 1995.

The Holy Bible. Revised Standard Version. New York, NY: Thomas Nelson & Sons, 1946.

Hurley, Joanna. *Mother Teresa: A Pictoral Biography*. Philadelphia, PA: Courage Books, 1997.

King, Martin Luther Jr. *Strength to Love*. Minneapolis, MN: Fortress Press, 1963.

Mandela, Nelson. *Long Walk to Freedom*. Essex, UK: Little Brown & Co., 1995.

St. Bonaventure. *Life of St. Francis*. Rockford, IL: Tan Books and Publishers, Inc., 1992.

Williamson, Marianne. *A Return to Love: Reflections on the Principles of a Course in Miracles*. New York, NY: Harper Collins, 1992.

Wintz, Jack. Lights: *Revelations of God's Goodness*. Cincinnati, OH: St. Anthony Messenger Press, 1996.

Web Sites

www.bartleby.com

www.catholic-forum.com/saints

www.ewtn.com/motherteresa/words.htm

www.Joan-of-Arc.org

www.petersnet.net/research/retrieve_full.cfm?RecNum=3080

Music

Gregorio Allegri, *Palestrina Missa Papae Marcelli*. Hamburg, Germany: Archiv Produktion, Polydore International GmbH, 1986.

Johannes Brahms, *A German Requiem, op. 45*. Hamburg, Germany: Polydor International GmbH, 1964.

Sarah Brightman, *Fly*. Hamburg, Germany: EastWest Productions GmbH, 1996.

Mariah Carey, *Daydream*. New York, NY: Columbia Records, 1995.

City of Angels, *City of Angels*. Burbank, CA: Warner Bros., 1998.

Robert Haig Coxon, *The Silent Path*. Westmount, Quebec, Canada: R.H.C. Productions Inc., 1995.

Dario G., *Sun Machine*. New York, NY: Kinetic Records, 1998.

Celine Dion, *Celine Dion*. New York, NY: Columbia and Sony Music Entertainment, 1997.

Bill Douglas, *Deep Peace*. San Francisco, CA: Hearts of Space, 1996.

Peter Gabriel, *Passion*. Los Angeles, CA: Geffen Records, 1989.

Lisa Gerrard, *The Mirror Pool*. Los Angeles, CA: 4AD, 1995.

Chloe Goodchild, *Devi*. Red Bank, NJ: Raven Recording, 1996.

James Horner, *Braveheart*. London, England: Decca Record Company Limited, 1995.

Jars of Clay, *Jars of Clay*. New York, NY: Brentwood Music Inc., 1995.

Trevor Jones and Randy Edelman. *The Last of the Mohicans*. Los Angeles, CA: Morgan Creek Music Group, 1992.

Madonna, *GHV2*. Burbank, CA: Warner Brothers, 2001.

Martika, *Martika's Kitchen*. New York, NY: Columbia Records, 1991.

Ennio Morricone, *The Mission*. Mississauga, Ontario, Canada: Virgin Records Ltd., 1986.

Ozzy Osbourne, *Ozzmosis*. New York, NY: Sony Music Entertainment, Inc., 1995.

Giovanni Pierluigi da Palestrina, *Missa de Beata Virgine*. Japan: Hungaroton, 1976.

Pointer Sisters, *Pointer Sisters Greatest Hits*. New York, NY: BMG Music, 1989.

Abraxas Pool, *Abraxas Pool*. Seattle, WA: Miramar Productions, 1997.

Raphael, *Music to Disappear In*. San Francisco, CA: Hearts of Space, 1988.

Savage Garden, *Savage Garden*. New York, NY: Columbia Records, 1997.

Styx, *Edge of the Century*. Hollywood, CA: A & M Records, Inc., 1990.

L. Subramaniam, *Baraka*. New York, NY: BMG Music, 1992.

Tina Turner, *Simply the Best*. Hollywood, CA: Capitol Records, 1991.

U2, *Rattle and Hum*. Los Angeles, CA: Polygram Records, 1990.

Vangelis, *1492 Conquest of Paradise*. New York, NY: Atlantic Recording Corporation, 1992.

Hans Zimmer and Lisa Gerrard, *Gladiator*. London, England: Decca Record Company Limited, 2000.